BEGIN

and Begin Again

ALSO BY
DENNY EMERSON

◆◆◆

How Good Riders Get Good
Know Better to Do Better

Denny Emerson

BEGIN

and Begin Again

The Bright Optimism
of Reinventing Life with Horses

TRAFALGAR SQUARE
North Pomfret, Vermont

First published in 2021 by
Trafalgar Square Books
North Pomfret, Vermont 05053

Disclaimer of Liability
The author and publisher shall have neither liability nor responsibility to any person or entity with respect to any loss or damage caused or alleged to be caused directly or indirectly by the information contained in this book. While the book is as accurate as the author can make it, there may be errors, omissions, and inaccuracies.

Trafalgar Square Books encourages the use of approved safety helmets in all equestrian sports and activities.

Library of Congress Cataloging-in-Publication Data
Names: Emerson, Denny, author.
Title: Begin and begin again : the bright optimism of reinventing life with
    horses.
Description: North Pomfret, Vermont : Trafalgar Square Books, 2021. |
    Includes index. | Summary: "In his third book, renowned horseman Denny
    Emerson once again masterfully intertwines his entertaining reflections
    from a life embedded in the equestrian world with serious philosophical
    questions faced by the industry today and practical advice honed by his
    immense experience. Here he explores all the different ways we begin a
    life with horses, or begin it over again, and how that constant
    reinvention is integral to our ability to keep horses a part of our
    lives over time"-- Provided by publisher.
Identifiers: LCCN 2021031933 (print) | LCCN 2021031934 (ebook) | ISBN
    9781646010394 (paperback) | ISBN 9781646010400 (epub)
Subjects: LCSH: Horsemanship--Psychological aspects.
Classification: LCC SF309 E63 2021 (print) | LCC SF309 (ebook) | DDC
    798.2--dc23
LC record available at https://lccn.loc.gov/2021031933
LC ebook record available at https://lccn.loc.gov/2021031934

All photographs courtesy of Denny Emerson *except:* p. 1 (skumer/Adobe Stock); p. 16 (Terri Cage /Adobe Stock); p. 42 (Rhett Savoie); p. 43 (Rebecca Didier); p. 67 (horsemen/Adobe Stock); p. 68 (Talitha/Adobe Stock); p. 97 *inset* (clixphoto.com); p. 114 (Stefan Voegeli/Adobe Stock); p. 131 (Lindle Sutton); p. 161 (Kendall Szumilas); p. 171 (Ashley Neuhof); p. 176 (Melissa A. Priblo Chapman); p. 193 (Leslie Ellis)

Book design by *Katarzyna Misiukanis–Celińska (https://misiukanis-artstudio.com)*
Cover design by *RM Didier*
Index by *Andrea M. Jones (www.jonesliteraryservice.com)*
Typefaces: *Eskorte Latin*, *Impact*, *Metropolis* and *Lato*

Printed in China

10 9 8 7 6 5 4 3 2 1

To May Emerson

*who, sooner rather than later,
understood what it means
to be a horsewoman.*

CONTEN

Begin and Begin Again

TS

Acknowledgments

Special appreciation, once again, to the linguistics, grammar, and editing experts who created the finished product from the raw manuscript stage, including my my friend, Strafford, Vermont, neighbor and editor Anne Adams, and the crew at Trafalgar Square Books in North Pomfret, Vermont: Caroline Robbins, Martha Cook, Rebecca Didier, Kim Cook, Amy Wilson, Lizzie Gray, Marilyn Tobin, and freelance designer Katarzyna Misiukanis-Celińska.

If it takes a village to raise a child;
it takes a small city to publish a book.
My gratitude and thanks.

– Denny Emerson–

◆ ◆ ◆

You can't go back and change the beginning,
but you can start where you are
and change the ending.

C.S. Lewis

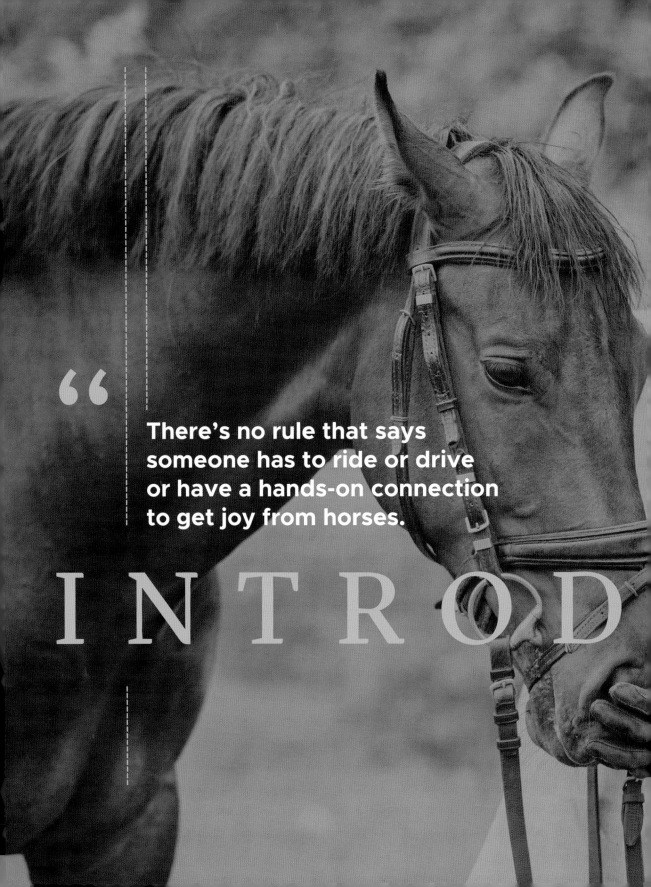

"

There's no rule that says someone has to ride or drive or have a hands-on connection to get joy from horses.

INTROD

_ Three, Two, One

Without conscious intent, I wrote a backward trilogy. My first book about riding is called *How Good Riders Get Good*. It is based on my decades of upper-level competing, and it's oriented toward those readers who might want more insight into what goes into becoming an elite rider.

The book deals with how all sorts of small, medium, and big choices—some made almost daily and without much thought—can lead either toward or away from riding goals.

Then, a few years later, I wrote a second book, *Know Better to Do Better*. This book has a broader and more diverse aim, and in many instances, I discuss strategies

UCTION

and training techniques that I would now go back and do differently if I had one of those magical "do-over" buttons. I talked about various horses, how I worked with them, and how I would do it differently if I had a second chance with them.

This, the third book, *Begin and Begin Again*, was triggered by the realization that we actually *do* have that "do-over" button, and it is right here, right now, at our fingertips, and all we have to do is choose to push the button.

Henry David Thoreau ended *Walden* with these famous words: *"Only that day dawns to which we are awake. There is more day to dawn. The sun is but a morning star."* Each new dawn offers an opportunity for a new beginning, if only we are awake enough to be aware. Too often, I think, we are caught up in what we did yesterday, and the day before that, which can hide the possibilities of positive change.

I wrote this third book of my backward trilogy to explore the ways to turn those hidden possibilities into realities.

Much like my riding career over the past 70 years—full of zigs and zags, twists and turns—this book is not one that has a beginning, a middle, and an end. This book is about the many ways we can start out with horses, each one as valid as any other—so long as we don't hurt the horse—and then, as our circumstances change, how we can reinvent or revisit that association.

_ That Little Prefix

There is power and potential in the little prefix "re."

The primary definitions of "re" that I found by consulting various dictionaries include "again," "once more," "afresh," "anew," and "back to an original place."

Now there are a few "re" words that have negative connotations, such as "retire" and "retreat," but most of them possess the hope of doing something over, only this time, doing it better: Restore, revive, reinvigorate, renew, repair, reinvent, and revitalize are some of the optimistic ways of using the "re" prefix.

Sure, we have the choice to retreat. We may even retire. But doing so does not preclude the chance to reinstate our fixation with horses, perhaps in some different form, but true to the original passion.

Remember what Yogi Berra said when his baseball team was far behind an opponent? "It ain't over 'til it's over." Even that line has been modified to, "It ain't over 'til it's over, and even then, it ain't necessarily over."

The horses aren't going anywhere...

_ No Rules

There's no rule that says someone has to ride or drive or have a hands-on connection to get joy from horses. Some paint horses, others take photos of horses; some sponsor a young rider, work with horse-rescue organizations, build saddles, or write horse books. Others read horse books, and still others have horses as pasture pets and never ride them but get a great deal of pleasure from the company of their horses and from just taking care of them.

The only person you have to please in this is yourself.

This book is an attempt to talk about the many options and pursuits in the horse world. You can read it from start to finish, or you can dip in and read the parts that relate to your particular situation.

It's easy to get caught up in the idea that the pyramid shape is the way to visualize horse sports and other ways of relating to horses—that there's a big base supporting the tip, which represents an elite handful. How much better, I think, not to drink that Kool-Aid. Any part of the pyramid is as valid as any other part.

If it satisfies you to reach for some sort of championship status, strive away. If you find satisfaction, and peace and serenity, perhaps, in sitting on a bale of hay on a winter's night, listening to your horse munch hay, then sit and listen.

I'll say it again: It only matters if it matters to you. ◈ ◆ ◆

BEGIN

for the First Time

Everyone starts out with horses from somewhere, and for me, that somewhere was Exeter, New Hampshire, when I was seven or eight, and it didn't even involve actual live horses.

1

... Starting Out

Everyone starts out with horses from somewhere, and for me, that somewhere was Exeter, New Hampshire, when I was seven or eight, and it didn't even involve actual live horses.

Back then, before television, there were cowboy radio shows: Tom Mixx, Gene Autry, Roy Rogers, and my favorite, *The Lone Ranger*.

I had an old radio with a wooden frame, and some sort of parchment-like speaker that would vibrate and distort the sounds. It made no difference to me. I'd come home from the Exeter Day School, go up to my room, and listen to the *William Tell Overture* announcing the arrival of the masked man of the plains on his great white stallion Silver.

I was infatuated with the idea of horses even before I had any experience with a living horse.

There were also kids' horse books, but, better still, because of the pictures, were cowboys and indians comic books.

There was no such thing as English riding in my imaginary horse world, because all the heroes lived in the West and rode palomino or silver or coal-black stallions, who, apparently, never walked or trotted, but lived their entire lives at the fast gallop.

It's a mistake to underestimate the power of the imaginary world of radio, books, movies, and TV to paint a picture that begins the horse addiction. Later, access to the real thing only adds to an existing condition, which, like malaria, resists any hope of cure.

_ Can I Have a Pony?

In 1950, the summer that I would turn nine, my family moved from Exeter, where there weren't any horses that I ever saw, to the campus of the Stoneleigh-Prospect Hill School for Girls, in Greenfield, Massachusetts. From the back door of our house to a barn full of real horses was about a 30-second walk. The school barn was literally in our back yard.

The barn had a big sliding front door that opened to a whitewashed barn with a cement floor. Just to the right was the door to the tack room. The next door on the same side opened to a grain room with bins. Then there were four box stalls. The entire left-hand side of the barn began with several box stalls, beyond which were six or seven straight stalls, also known as standing stalls, for the lesson horses.

At the far end of the horse section of the long barn aisle were two white bat-wing swinging doors that divided the horses from the cows. In the cow barn, there were rows of stanchions on both sides of the center aisle, a corridor leading to the milk room, and stairs to the vast hay loft.

The reason for the cows at a girls' boarding school was that during World War II, which had ended just four years earlier, as part of the national war effort, many

_ Never write off or underestimate the power of comic books over the pliable minds of impressionable kids. I listened to *The Lone Ranger* and Gene Autry and Roy Rogers on the radio. I saw them in vivid action in comic books, to the point where my first riding goal was to gallop fast while shooting someone. Disclaimer: I was eight. ▲

schools had gardens or small farms to create a degree of self-sustainability. Down at one end of the big hay field were the remnants of what had been a pig pen.

All this—the barn, the hay fields, trucks, tractor, horses, cows, a wood lot, pig pens—created a rural atmosphere in what was also then a rural town in a mostly rural part of Massachusetts. Having horses grew naturally from the general environment, far different from now, in 2021, when farm life has been pushed to the outskirts of US society.

At age nine, just entering fourth grade at Four Corners School, I wasn't instantly involved with riding. Horses, yes; riding, no. I was small, the horses were big, and these were horses ridden in English tack. My heroes were cowboys.

When I say, "Horses, yes," I mean I lived in that barn, in the front horse section, the farther milk-cow end, in the hayloft, playing and making forts, becoming aware of livestock through osmosis. I watched as the horses got shod. I watched the veterinarian tube worm with a bucket of rank-smelling, pasty-white worm medicine. I cleaned stalls, helped in the summers with haying, and rode in the back of the big farm truck when Francis Kinsman would drive to the lumber yard in Bernardston to get sawdust.

Without conscious awareness, I was learning how it worked to handle and take care of horses and cows.

In the summer of 1952, when I was ten years old, about to turn eleven in August, I saw a classified ad in the back of the local paper, *The Greenfield Recorder Gazette*. It read something like, "Just in. New load of ponies and horses. Some nice ones. Call Louis Goodyear, Sunderland, Mass."

Sunderland was minutes from Greenfield. I started in on my parents, just the way kids always do. "Can I have a pony? I want a pony. I need a pony. Can we go look at those ponies?"

_ The Stoneleigh Prospect Hill School barn, a 30-second walk from my house, was home to lots of "barn rats"—kids who loved to be immersed in the world of horses and who learned by osmosis what taking care of horses required. I started to work toward my Barn Rat Diploma in 1950. Here, in 1956, riding Lippitt Sandy bareback, I am probably in the equivalent of Barn Rat High School. ▼

So at some point, my parents gave in and drove south on Route 5, through Deerfield, turned left across the Connecticut River into Sunderland and left again after the bridge, into the smorgasbord of horses and ponies that was Louis Goodyear's sales barn.

I didn't know how to ride because, except for maybe a couple of times sitting on a horse, I'd never ridden. But I'd watched plenty of Westerns, so I figured I knew enough to handle a pony. Kids don't know that they can't, so often it turns out that they can. Adult self-doubt comes later.

Louis watched me ride one sort of "sharp" bay pony, and he could see that I was a greenie, so he brought out a little black-and-white pinto. "This is a kid-broke hoss," he said. I got on, and I somehow knew how to ride him.

My parents bought Paint, with a little Western saddle, a silver-mounted breastplate and bridle, and a Navajo saddle pad for $250. And that started it for me, the riding part, after a long non-riding apprenticeship.

Denny Emerson | *Begin and Begin Again*

So that was my first start with horses. I say "first start" because over many decades since Paint, I have restarted, and recalibrated and reinvented my life with horses many times, in many ways, but I know that was my first.

We all have that first time. Mine happened to be pretty unsophisticated and without lessons, what I think of as a backyard kind of beginning.

Let's look at other ways to begin, because life circumstances will vary all over the lot, and these will drive either opportunities or lack of opportunities, which in turn will make access to horses easy as in my case, or hard, or impossible until or unless the opportunities change.

_ Finding Your Way

Probably the easiest and smoothest way to get involved with horses is by being born into a family that already has horses, is supportive, and can afford them. That way, if the horse bug bites you, you are already there, with the entire support network established. You can learn from the ground up, top down, sideways, every which way, and you will learn without even knowing that you are learning just from day-to-day living it. In my first book, *How Good Riders Get Good*, there are a number of rider profiles, and in several of these cases, the good riders had family support from the very start.

Not every child who grows up with instant and easy availability to horses becomes interested. It is one of life's ironies that this child, who has a horse world laid out at her feet, has zero interest, while that child over there, with no access or support, is mesmerized by horses. We see this constantly.

Another way to get access to horses if your family isn't interested is to have a friend who has horses, and who is willing to share with you. This isn't as good as having your

Starting Over: Stories from Re-Riders

Irene van Vessem

I grew up in apartments with non-riding parents. Where did my love of horses come from? No idea. I took on odd jobs as a kid to pay for riding lessons. Later, my husband didn't ride, and we had city jobs and other interests. That's life.

In 2010 I took early retirement and thought, *Before I get too old, I'll do one week's desert ride in Tunisia, kind of a "farewell to horses."* And it was fantastic. Back home my husband said, "Why don't we buy a small farm and have horses now?" He didn't even ride then. Love him. We did it. We've got our farm, four horses, switched to Western, made new friends, go on trail rides. We're 66 and 69.

To be continued. ◆

All across the world of horses, every weekend, there will be horseback riding clinics given in all the various types of riding, and there will also be driving clinics, and specialty clinics. Clinics can be "doors" to new beginnings. The usual way that this works is for a stable, a group, a school or college with a riding club to decide to host a clinic, either as a fundraising venture, as a way of bringing expertise to a local area, or some combination of these and other reasons.

Between a lesson and a clinic, there's not much difference for those riders who treat the clinic as a lesson, who show up 30 minutes before, ride, untack, and leave. They just had an expensive lesson, maybe a few things phrased differently, but basically, they missed the point.

Think of a lesson, just about any lesson from any teacher, as one little stepping stone toward something bigger. You come in, ride for maybe an hour, get told a few things, get shown a few things, and off you go to practice until the next lesson. You may be working on your position on the flat. You may be working on not bouncing at the sitting trot. You may be trying to feel that elusive adjustable canter. Whatever it is you are working on during that one-hour lesson, you can bet you are not going

When I was a student at Dartmouth College in Hanover, New Hampshire, from 1959 to 1963, there was no college riding program. Now there is, and here I am giving a mini-clinic to some Dartmouth students a couple of years ago. Unlike most clinics, my day-rate (free) was cheap! ▼

Denny Emerson | *Begin and Begin Again*

10

to learn it to the point of owning it in any given session. Maybe you'll start to grasp it in a month or two—maybe, more likely, in nine months to a year—but one single lesson, or two of them, are just a drop or two in a big bucket.

Now a clinic, when it is taught by a good teacher, will not be just a lesson, and especially not just a lesson for the riders who combine their sessions with all the other sessions by intently watching for hours over the course of the clinic. Here's why: a clinician will usually be a successful rider or trainer, who, over years, has developed a system of training. That system will be a compilation of concepts, theories, techniques, and strategies, each of which will be made up of hundreds of stepping stones, leading to something bigger. A good clinician will do far more than teach some lessons. The best clinicians will try to explain concepts, theories, techniques, and strategies, which the good student will write down in a notebook, just exactly as though being taught in a college lecture.

Then, the good student, in collaboration with her own "normal" teacher, will, through many individual lessons, each one a stepping stone, begin to use the concepts brought by the clinician to broaden her greater understanding of the overall process.

If you go to a clinic for diversion, to fool around with your friends, to chatter and gossip, to let your attention drift in and out, do not be surprised if two weeks after the clinic, you can't remember much of what it was about.

There are learners and there are non-learners. It's up to you. ◆

own, but you can get used to being around living horses, which is lots better access than reading about them or watching movies.

But of all the ways to get involved with horses—and riding—the paid-for riding lesson is the most common. Where does someone get riding lessons? Here, there, and everywhere. From local riding stables. From summer camps. From dude ranches. From school and college programs. From lavish, high-dollar lesson barns to run-down stables where you trade stall mucking for the chance to ride. What you can get will depend upon what you can afford, and what you are willing to do if you want it badly enough when money is tight.

There's a phrase that I hear all the time, "It must be nice…"

It must be nice to live on a farm. It must be nice to have your own horse. It must be nice to be able to show—to take lessons—to have a truck and trailer—to go to train with Joe Schmoe—to do this, that, and whatever. And, yes, it is nice. And if you can do it, and can afford it, you start with an advantage. Don't let others embarrass you with the guilt game but *do* utilize those advantages; don't squander them.

And for those not so lucky in this way, there's a choice. Spend time and energy in envy and jealousy, or figure out other ways to make it work.

It's not such an easy task to learn whether a riding teacher is what we might term "valid."

Even at the college level, where most of the professors have advanced degrees, there

| 1 | Begin for the First Time

11

Field Notes
The Stiller the Hands

... Hands hold the reins. Reins lead to the bit. The bit is in the horse's mouth. The horse has a sensitive and "vulnerable" mouth. It makes sense, does it not, to have soft, elastic, sympathetic, following hands? It's a quest that never ends—the "good hands" journey. ▼

An old barn-repair analogy says that you fix a sagging roofline by first fixing the foundation. This equally applies to the way the best instructors—like Klaus Balkenhol, Sally Swift, Louise Nathorst, Walter Christensen, Richard Shrake, Gayle Lampe, and Lynn Palm—are apt to address a rider issue.

Say that a rider has erratic control of her hands. They post when she posts, or they are never steady or consistent, whatever. Instead of just saying, "Stop letting your hands move," trainers like these will look for the deeper root cause.

Perhaps they will notice that her seat is erratic. How can you have steady hands with a floppy seat? But instead of working on her seat, they will

Denny Emerson | *Begin and Begin Again*

look even deeper. Why is her seat erratic? Well, she is tight in her lower back, to the point that it creates a lack of flexibility in her pelvis. But why is she tight in her lower back?

Well, she is trying so hard to "sit up, shoulders back," that it is freezing her entire torso. (I am making up this sequence to give an idea of possible problems and possible solutions.)

So these great instructors might start to fix the hand problem by working on her posture problem, which helps her stiffness problem, which helps her develop a more flexible pelvis, which will allow her to develop a more independent seat, which will (finally) help address the erratic hands.

This is so much different than what the greener instructor might do by concentrating on her hands. The best trainers dig down to find the root problem, repair that first, and then build back up. ◆

... Most riders have taken a riding lesson. Many riders have taken dozens of lessons. Some have taken hundreds of lessons, even thousands, over many decades. People will ask, "How come you still take lessons? I thought you knew how to ride." Those questioners will not have heard the saying that to learn how to ride well takes two lifetimes. Here, Abby Emerson is in a lesson given by Emily Fabiano. ▲

will be a wide diversity of teaching competence. Some brilliant scholar with a PhD might be pedantic and boring, while a young instructor might have the students on the edge of their chair. How, then, does someone rate a riding teacher at some random stable in some random town in some random state, when there are no types of uniform certification to even hint at some level of competence? And for that matter, what does the word "valid" mean? There are so many different types and styles of riding, so many competing ideas about what constitutes correct training, that what one group might term valid, as in orthodox and correct, some other group might condemn as the near cousin of horse abuse.

_ Options to Consider

So, if you are a parent looking for lessons for your child, or if you are an adult beginner thinking about getting

Starting Over: Stories from Re-Riders

KIM HENDERSON

I was 19 and went to a "hack stable," as they called them 40-some years ago. I went trail riding every Sunday, although the terror I felt beforehand would have discouraged most people.

On a whim I went to see a horse for sale, an ex-barrel and reining horse named Dusty. I saw this most beautiful Palomino mare and she walked toward me and that was it. I knew nothing about riding. She came to me in the back of an open pickup truck, to a stable near my home.

She was just what you would think of as a barrel racer, and I was terrified to ride her. I had her 21 years until she died at 35. She is buried on the farm I eventually bought. She taught me how to ride and was the best friend anyone could ever have and a true beauty inside and out. I still miss her after 20 years. ◆

started yourself, what are some strategies? It seems to me that your very first challenge is to decide what sort of riding you are interested in, because many later decisions will depend upon that choice.

In the United States, I would think that the biggest division among riding disciplines is whether someone rides English, with one general type of saddle, or Western, with an entirely different type of saddle.

Within both general English and Western styles are all sorts of sub-types of riding. In English riding, one main divide is whether you do or do not want to jump. If you do want to jump, you are probably looking at the disciplines called eventing, show jumping, show hunter, hunt seat equitation, foxhunting, and racing over fences.

If jumping doesn't interest you, non-jumping disciplines include dressage, saddle seat, trail riding, both competitive trail and endurance (you can also use a Western saddle for all sorts of trail riding), polo, and general pleasure riding.

If Western is your main choice, there are lots of options, such as reining, cutting, ranch work, barrel racing, and rodeo.

So before you plunge into a very big pool of options, it probably makes sense to learn how these styles differ from one another. Maybe you have a friend who does working cow horse. You've gone to some of her competitions and you are already interested in that sport. Or you have watched some local horse shows and you think that show jumping looks like fun. In other words, you are not plunging into the entire pool, but into some part that already grabs your interest.

Something else to consider: How big are you into risk-taking? Do you like to ride your bike down steep hills with no hands on the handlebars or jump off high rocks into the pool below, or are you much happier

walking your dog in a flower-strewn meadow? Because if you get yourself into the wrong horse sport for your personal psychological profile, you can wind up bored to death or scared to death, and the best time to avoid that is before you begin. Some horse sports are fast, furious, and dangerous. Some are slow, calm, and relatively safe. Many find some middle between extremes. Find out which is which. Ask around. Go and watch. Be aware. Not all kinds of riding are similar. Much quiet discontent and even, truth be told, misery, can be avoided by choosing the sport that fits who you fundamentally are. Sure, you can always change later, but it only makes sense to scope it out before you leap.

But for whatever reason, wise, foolish, well thought out, or impulsive, you have decided that you want to learn about a specific type of riding. Now we get back to our initial questions: Does this riding teacher know what she is doing? Is she a good teacher? Will I learn from her the things that I need to know?

Rule No. 1: Watch her teach at least one lesson. Does she seem bright or bored? Is her style gentle or militaristic? Is she able to make clear and logical comments? Do you have the sense that your child, or you, would get along with her?

If that fits, how do you as a "greenie" know that she is teaching valid material? Short answer—you probably can't. But you can ask around, have someone you respect watch her teach your lesson, perhaps watch clinics in the same sort of riding by some well-known riders, and mentally compare what they say to what she says.

_ A Visit to a Horse Farm

I don't mean to compare apples to oranges. If I visit a breeding farm in Lexington, Kentucky, owned by an oil sheikh from Dubai, and I see manicured flower beds, fountains, and chandeliers, I shouldn't mentally contrast that opulence with my visit to a local boarding and teaching facility in Anywhere, USA. Glitz doesn't necessarily equate with excellence or competence, but neither should the local barn be a mess of broken fencing, cobwebs, and dirt on the cushions of the tack-room couch.

If you are going to check out various places that are on your list of possible lesson barns, what might you realistically expect to see, or, conversely, hope not to see?

Well, to be blunt about it, horses are destructive and messy. They chew the boards in their paddocks, they churn up mud, they create piles of manure that get churned up in that mud. They happily roll in the muck. They tear their blankets and scatter hay everywhere, to the point that the poor barn owner feels like the proverbial "one step forward, two steps backward." This is a reality unknown to the wealthy owners of show places, with large staffs of paid workers, and just because you will see some surface chaos and mess doesn't mean that the basics are poor at a local barn.

So look more deeply. There are certain characteristics that signal good basic horsemanship, and these you will hope to see.

Is the barn aisle a safe space? Is it fairly neat and free from junk and obstacles like wheelbarrows, manure forks, half-open hay bales, trash, and litter? Now, be real here. If you come in the middle of a busy day, and you see dirt on the floor, bridles on wall hooks and dirty gear on hangers in the tack room, that may often be irrelevant, because a busy trainer without a big work squad can't grab a broom every other minute to sweep the aisle. At the end of the day, the place may be neat as a pin.

Look further. Are the stalls fairly tidy, or half full of manure? Are the water buckets full of clear-looking water, or are they foul and smelly, half full of green scum? Do you see bale string mixed into the mud in the paddocks?

A farmer was sitting on his tractor, his well-kept farm in the background, when a neighbor stopped by. "George," he said, "Your farm looks so good it could run itself." "Sure would," replies George. "Downhill." A farm, a barn, left to their own devices, slide into chaos, dirt, and disrepair. Look at the barn aisle for much of what you need to know about how the riding facility is managed. ▲

Are there bits and pieces of tack lying around, peppermint wrappers, McDonald's cups—a general lack of a tidy mindset?

What about the tack room? This will be the place where you will warm up on a chilly day, or clean tack. Is it dirty or clean? Are dogs lying on the furniture getting dirt on the places where humans sit? Is there the stench of dirty cat litter?

Now, what about a bathroom? I was at a farm years ago in the Midwest, teaching a clinic. A man came out of the public toilet and said, "That place would gag a maggot." Again, I don't wish to imply that every local barn should rival the five-star hotel atmosphere of some dot-com billionaire's show place, but there's no excuse for a filthy tack room or a disgusting bathroom.

What about the general atmosphere? Is there a loud blaring radio? Lots of yelling, even swearing? Are kids running around, maybe spooking the horses, or is there a general sense of quiet, respectful horsemanship?

The lesson itself can be incredibly revealing. Is the teacher sympathetic and methodical, or loud and bombastic, negative, and critical? I'm not talking about warranted emphasis, which can involve a raised voice, even shouting when outdoors, but I am talking about a general tone.

And here's a turnoff: Does the teacher keep looking at her phone during the lesson? That's a sure sign that her attention is elsewhere, don't you think?

I would not expect a prospective student to be aware of various schools of thought about training techniques, or nuances or subtleties of performance. On the other hand, I would expect that the prospective customer could differentiate between calm teaching and rough use of hands, whip, and spur.

The place you choose to learn will shape your attitude, or the attitude of your child, toward much else in the world of horses. Doesn't it make sense to perform due diligence before you decide where to land?

Barn Rats

If you missed the chance to be a barn rat at age 11, and you are now 31 or 51 or 71, it's not too late to get your Barn Rat A-1 Certification. You just need to go and hang around a barn. That's it. No experience necessary, because the essence of being a barn rat is that you learn as you go.

There's no specific course of study leading to a Barn Rat Diploma. Neither is there any particular time period or number of study hours that you are required to fulfill. You can do it only on weekends or evenings or during your vacation. And while some barn rats get actual lessons, the majority learn by osmosis—by watching, listening, helping out, and absorbing.

There are hundreds of examples. Here's one: A horse gets brought to a set of cross-ties, and he gets his feet picked out. You watch how the handler gets him to lift his front feet. Then you watch the way she uses the hoof pick to dig out the dirt or manure from around the frog. If it's winter, and his feet are clogged with ice, you'll see how she may use a hammer to break the ice ball free. Then you'll see how she gets the horse to lift his hind feet. You'll observe the careful ways she avoids getting kicked. You will see how she holds his hind leg across her thigh.

All these things that you did not know, you start to learn how to do:

- How to brush a tail without pulling out tail hairs.

- How to train a horse to face you when you are about to let him go in a paddock so he doesn't kick you.

- How to put on and take off his blanket.

- How to never leave the handles of a wheelbarrow sticking out for a horse to get tangled in.

- How to approach a horse from behind so as not to startle him.

- How to dump grain from a pail into his feed tub without getting bitten or having him lunge at you.

- How to soak beet pulp.

- How to handle bale string after opening a bale of hay.

Denny Emerson | *Begin and Begin Again*

- How to use a sweat scraper.

- How much hay to feed at any given feeding.

- How to pick out a stall.

- How to check a water bucket to see if the water is fresh and clean.

- How to put up the stirrups of an English saddle after you dismount.

- How to wash a horse around his head without getting water in his eyes or ears.

- How to clean a bridle and saddle.

- How all the pieces of a bridle fit together.

- How to safely catch a horse.

- How to safely lead a horse.

- How to saddle and bridle a horse.

- How to clean a horse before and after he gets worked.

- How to spot moldy hay in an open bale.

- How to check the girth to see that it is tight enough but not too tight.

- How to pull a mane.

- How to tell if a horse has heat or filling in a leg.

- How to cold-hose a horse's leg.

- How to know if an injury or illness is so bad that you need to call the vet RIGHT NOW.

Everywhere you look, there's another article or blog about the decline of "horsemanship." And we don't have to look deeply to see the source of the dilemma. When I got my first pony in 1952, I kept him in the little red former chicken house in my back yard, about a 20-second walk from my house. Today, chances are, if I were a typical American kid, I would live in a suburb, and my pony would live in a barn within driving distance, perhaps 3 to 15 miles away, give or take.

Today's little horse-crazy kid wants just as badly as we did then to spend all day every day in the barn, but circumstances prevent barn-rat-ism. Someone else feeds the pony, turns the pony out, brings the pony in, cleans his stall, makes sure he has clean water, holds him for the vet and the farrier, does all the things that kids who had instant access used to do.

— A barn rat is a human who lives in a barn, in a jumping ring, in a dressage arena, and who learns by osmosis, forward, backward, upward, downward, every which way about horses, from top to bottom. You have to live it to own it. There's no getting around that truth. ▼

Denny Emerson | *Begin and Begin Again*

And sure, let's talk about being able to pack a picnic lunch and head off riding for the day on Saturday. Today, if a car didn't hit you in the first five minutes, some weirdo from the frightening detective show *Criminal Minds* would come by in his white serial-killer van... good luck with that one!

So how can horsemanship stay vital when the horse is one place and the horse owner or rider is some other place, and maybe, with luck, they interact for seven or eight hours a week, or often, for a shorter time than that? Hard to fix this sort of reality. ◆

- How to call 911 in case someone gets hurt or there's a fire or other emergency.

- How to tell 911 the correct address.

- How and what to feed barn cats.

- How to clean the barn toilet so it doesn't become a gross mess.

- How to tell all the horses apart.

- How to sweep the barn aisle.

- How to make sure that you have the right bridle for the right pony or horse.

- How to begin to tell one breed of horse from another by their appearance.

- How to stack hay.

- How to bed down a stall.

As you can see, there are many, many details, large and small, that all good horsemen and horsewomen understand. Being a barn rat puts you right where you need to be to learn them. The Greek philosopher Aristotle said, "For things we need to learn how to do before we can do them, we learn by doing them." It's the hands-on experience barn rats get that turns them into horse people. It's better than any classroom setting, more effective than any number of lectures. There are 15- and 16-year-old barn rats I would trust to oversee my whole place. If you want the best way to learn, become a barn rat. ◆ ◆ ◆

BEGIN
to Appreciate
the Here and Now

*While it is true that much of what
this book is about is the chance
for new beginnings, I should point
out how easy it can be to miss
the here and now, this day, this
experience, this ride, this horse.*

2

While it is true that much of what this book is about is the chance for new beginnings, I should point out how easy it can be to miss the here and now, this day, this experience, this ride, this horse.

It's a cliché that we have three places in which to live—the past, the present, and the future.

If the present is less than great, if the future looks no better—or worse, I suppose—it's okay to dwell in the past. We find this to be true with older people who endlessly reminisce about their time in college, 50 or 60 years earlier, or about horses they rode, jumps they cleared, championships they won. Bruce Springsteen wrote a song about this, "Glory Days." It's about those who constantly recall former times, earlier victories. And if this is all that someone has, if those places in time are pretty much all that's left—their only bright and beautiful refuge—why not support them there? Ask about those former experiences, encourage them, be kind. Someday, maybe someone will do it for you.

Field Notes
Hidden Messages

What are some of the hidden messages in this photo of two walking horses? An athlete does not just become an athlete like manna from heaven. Underpinning athletic performance is base fitness. Base fitness doesn't float down from above like autumn leaves. You have to put it there.

And before you can put hard work there, you need to put lots of easy work there first, so that the hard work doesn't create injuries. And that means lots of walking. It means that the good trainers don't leave the horse standing around for days, and then go ride it hard. Good trainers are consistent. They are base builders and basics builders first. Only then do they layer on more training.

So that's one message: walk your horse into fitness before and during the rest of the process. It's good for the body, good for the mind.

Another message: many trainers farm out the "boring" work to working students or other employees. I mean, what the heck, anybody can walk a horse, right?

_ There is a saying: "You can't hurt a horse at a walk." But you CAN turn a weak horse into a strong horse with lots of walking. It is a secret hidden in plain sight. ▼

Denny Emerson | *Begin and Begin Again*

Yes and no. The trainers who get on, do a session of flat work or jump through some gymnastic lines, only to then hand the horse off to someone else do not know what happens next, nor do they get to know the horse as well as someone who does all the riding, nor does the horse get familiar and comfortable being ridden by that person.

The trainer who has by now hopped on one or more other horses in a string doesn't know whether the trusted rider puts in the entire time at an active walk, or if she lets the horse sort of slop along at three miles an hour. The trainer won't know how the horse deals with mud, stream crossings, terrain, flapping plastic, you name it.

Some months later, flying along on cross-country at some event, all of that might be irrelevant, or the lack of a deeper partnership may be revealed.

Why take that chance? You need to know your horse. Even more key: your horse has to know and trust you, and not only inside some ring. ◆

But don't dwell in the past just for the sake of avoiding the possibilities of what you can be doing today and tomorrow, not if you are still able to get up in the morning and put on your socks. The future is going to happen regardless of what you do, so you can dwell in the past, talk about what you are going to do tomorrow or next year, or you can decide to get something done today, this day, right now.

This is a book about horses, so let's decide what you can do today with the horse you already ride.

First things first. Are you going to ride today or are you going to avoid riding today? If you are looking for an excuse *not* to ride today, maybe this is a good time to look at why you either won't or can't. Because there are reasons and excuses, and it may make sense to figure out which is which.

Here are some reasons why you are not going to ride today: *I am sick. I am recovering from an injury. I am on a business trip. My child is sick, and I have to take care of him. This is crunch week at my job and I have to work late. I am visiting my parents in Florida.*

All of those are reasons, rather than excuses. They are statements of fact.

Now let's come up with some excuses: *It's cold outside. It is hot outside. It is raining. It is snowing. I am tired. I am having a bad day at work. I am in a fight with my boyfriend. I don't feel like riding. I need a drink. I don't like my horse. I had a bad lesson yesterday.*

And so on. Excuses are like clouds in the sky, you can always find one if you look.

One of the main reasons that you do need to ride today is because the more your horse is in his stall, or hangs out in his field, the less likely he will be fit and strong enough to handle the training he'll need to learn his job. One of the worst mistakes humans make with horses is to assume that because horses are so

| 2 | Begin to Appreciate the Here and Now

25

much bigger and faster and stronger than people, they don't need the same type of fitness preparation that is normal for human athletes.

What do we know about all human athletes in just about any type of sport, anywhere on Earth? What one thing? They train. And what does "train" mean? It starts with doing whatever it takes to get strength, agility, stamina, and endurance. This will usually include hiking, running, weight training—anything to build muscle, respiratory fitness, and cardiovascular efficiency. Who ever heard of an "unfit athlete"? Those two words don't belong together. An athlete, by definition, is strong and fit, and it doesn't make an iota of difference if we are talking about humans, dogs, horses, racing camels, or any other creature that's being asked to perform physical tasks.

So, just as we would not expect an unfit human to be much good at soccer, tennis, swimming, basketball, or track and field, neither should we think a horse can be both unfit and athletic.

Horses are bigger and stronger than humans, this is true. But horses suffer exactly the same ways unfit humans suffer when they are pushed beyond what their training has prepared them to handle. Horses sweat. They pant. Their hearts pound. Their muscles cramp and spasm. You have to understand the truth right here if you are ever going to amount to much as a horse trainer.

Here it is in black and white: "Do not ask a horse to do something that he has not first been made fit enough to do." To ignore this is the worst kind of bad horsemanship.

There's a stereotype of kids on various high school and college sports teams being drilled by their coaches to "run one more lap" around the field. And while at some point in the preparation of the horse we may ask him to gallop, we don't start out that way.

We start our conditioning program at the walk. By "walk," we don't mean stroll or amble, nor do we mean some frantic go-go-go. The walk that brings the most benefit is a marching, forward walk, where the horse drops his head and briskly covers ground. In trail riding, this is called the "get home in time for supper" walk. I use a Garmin time, speed, and distance watch, and a good resolute walk is something like 4 miles an hour on flat terrain. An amble is around 3 miles an hour. An okay walk will be about 3.6, 3.7, or 3.8 miles an hour.

In other words, if I go out for about one hour and I walk the entire ride, I expect to cover between 3.6 and 4 miles, assuming decent footing and fairly flat terrain. On steeper hills, the horse won't be able to maintain this fast pace, and we might cover between 3.2 and 3.5 miles. There are also cell phone apps that track all of this. If you are interested, you can find ways to keep on top of your workout.

Many riders don't appreciate how much fitness and strength they can build into their horses at the walk, and how the walk reduces the risk of injury. There's a saying that "it is hard to hurt a horse at the walk." That's not literally true, because too much of anything can create damage, but walking doesn't create the bad tears and breakdowns that happen at higher speeds, where there is far more impact and wrenching on tendons, ligaments, and muscles.

You can walk a horse into quite a high level of fitness if you have the place to do it and the willingness to spend the time, and you can accomplish this with assurance that you aren't going to hurt the horse in the process.

Think of this as base-building. Actual walking strengthens tendons, ligaments, muscles, and bones. It doesn't do as much for the heart and lungs, which need higher levels of exertion, but if the horse has a solid walking base, he is far less likely to get injured when he is asked for more pace.

Try not to shirk the long, slow miles before you begin faster work. If you can prevent just one injury, you can save months of rehab. Be smart. Take it slowly. Do it right.

_ Horse-Buying Trips

When it comes time to buy a horse, the grass is always greener on the other side of the fence. I think part of this is the allure of the unknown compared to the boredom of the too familiar. There's a saying, "No man is a hero to his butler."

Not that many of us have a butler, but I get the saying. If a person is familiar, even if the person is highly accomplished, the familiarity wipes away some of the luster.

This is why someone who lives in Georgia will fly to Michigan to look at horses while someone from Michigan will fly to Georgia. How could the best deals on the best horses possibly be sitting in my own neighborhood? There's sort of a standing joke, or truism, whatever one chooses to call it, that if someone from the United States flies to anywhere in Europe to look at horses, the person *will* find a horse. It's probably a psychological reality that when the looking process involves lots of planning and traveling, the impetus to find something takes on more urgency.

Another semi-truism about the horse-hunting expedition is that if you are the one who has a horse for sale, you don't want to be the first stop on the purchaser's itinerary. Even though your horse might be the nicest horse that the looker is going to see all week, the lack of a basis of comparison probably will drive her to want to see others and while she may get discouraged enough to come back to try your horse again, she just as easily might settle for some other horse.

So much of buying is based on a whim and impulse rather than on rational analysis. There are dozens of factors involved, and most of us aren't even aware of what they are, even as they are happening. You look at a bunch of horses with one seller, get back in the car, drive to another farm and look at several more. Now it's time for lunch, and the seller takes you down the road to a local pub. You're sitting there in an Irish pub (or German, or French, or whatever) and you are charmed by the atmosphere. You like the person who has the horse for sale. You liked the horse with the crooked blaze. Before you know it, or even know why, you have made an offer and sealed the deal.

These things happen in ways like this all the time. Did you wind up with the best horse for the best price? Maybe. Maybe not. But it's too late now.

This is not to suggest that all horse deals are based on whim or sudden impulse, because the more experience you have, the more likely you are to learn how the game is played.

In the fall of 1961, I was in the beginning of my junior year at Dartmouth College, and I used to go over to Hitching Post Farm in South Royalton, Vermont, to take jumping lessons from Joe McLaughlin. Joe ran a summer riding camp and one weekend he was going to look at some young Thoroughbreds at several New England racetracks to see about picking up a couple to make into camp horses. I went along for the experience and our first stop was at Rockingham Park in Salem, New Hampshire.

I can't remember what we saw, but there was nothing that Joe wanted.

Then we looked at several at Suffolk Downs in Boston, and once again, we left there empty handed.

Our last stop would be Lincoln Downs in Rhode Island, perhaps not a top-of-the-line racetrack. And on a chilly evening, with trash blowing across the empty parking lot and lights missing in many of the shed rows, it seemed a bleak and forlorn place to find a nice horse.

We located the shed row on the back side, and the trainer, who was also the owner, led out a big brown colt, three or four years old, shaggy, with a growing winter coat, a long scraggly mane, barefoot on three of his four hooves, skinny and rough.

It was by now dark, and by headlights we watched the owner jog the colt up and down on the chipped and broken macadam surface between rows of empty stalls.

I liked him. Joe liked him. Joe and the owner climbed into the owner's car to discuss particulars. After some time, Joe got out, came back to his car, and sat down.

"What happened?" I asked.

"He gave me a price of $800," Joe replied. "I said I couldn't do it."

"But, Joe," I said, "that looks like a nice colt."

"Wait," said Joe.

We sat in our dark car for several minutes. The lights came on in the seller's car, as he opened the door. Joe got out. The two men talked.

Joe got back into our car. "Got him for $400," he said.

_ Love of the Stereotype

Vermont is famous for maple syrup. So famous that if there were three bottles of maple syrup on a shelf in a store, one marked "New York Maple Syrup," another marked "Quebec Maple Syrup," and the third, "Vermont Maple Syrup," most buyers would choose the Vermont product. And yet Vermont shares a border with New York State, and it shares a border with the Canadian province of Quebec. The syrup in the three bottles might be from the same grove of maple trees, from trees growing a few feet apart from one another. Exactly the same maple syrup, no difference whatsoever except the difference that exists in the mind of the prospective buyer.

Would you buy a "New Hampshire Lobster" if you had a chance to buy a "Maine Lobster"? Yet the lobsters swim back and forth above some imaginary line on the ocean floor.

People will travel from Virginia to buy a horse in Vermont. People will travel from Vermont to buy a horse in Virginia. You hear people bragging, "I have an Irish horse." You examine the pedigree, and his ancestors are pure German Holsteiner lines. And you hear, "Australian Thoroughbreds are tougher and sounder than American Thoroughbreds," yet the same ancestors weave through the bloodlines of horses from both countries, thanks to the ease of horse transport by air, which lets a buyer obtain a yearling from the Saratoga, New York, sale one week, and have the colt standing in a New Zealand or Australian paddock 10 days later.

There are situations where stereotypes blend into reality. Here's an example from my own history of horse buying: I once went to look at some ranch-raised Thoroughbreds turned out in a rugged pasture outside the small town of Joliet, Montana. Now, even though the pedigrees of those youngsters were basically interchangeable with the pedigrees of a similar group of colts and fillies who'd grown up in some flat field in Massachusetts, I'd say the Montana-breds were probably "tougher" simply because of the terrain and weather conditions in which they'd grown up. It wasn't because they were "Montana-breds." It was because they were "Montana-raised."

This entire stereotype business is tricky, because while some stereotypes are blatantly false, others have at least some basis in reality.

_ The Glitz Factor

The colt that Joe McLaughlin bought for $400 in 1961—Pink Card, by Post Card out of Pink Bow—was a distress sale. Joe knew it, the owner knew it, and the price reflected it.

When my wife May and I would meet Tom and Jessie Alderson, years later, at the Billings, Montana, airport to go look at Thoroughbreds on various Montana and Wyoming ranches, most of those horses were a more modern-day equivalent of Pink Card. We'd see them in muddy fields on the Blackfeet Indian reservation, in feedlots, or tied to rusty trailers, and to get any sense of what might lie beneath the mud and the manure and

Starting Over: Stories from Re-Riders

SCARLETT LOYA

When I was a senior in college, I bought my first OTTB. I thought I had extensive knowledge in starting young horses, so restarting one would be easy!

After graduating, I became a working student with Denny Emerson at his farm in Vermont. I quickly learned that the past six months of my training should have been long, slow miles of hacks and teaching small "ABCs" to my mare. I had created holes in her training, intertwined with anxiety from being at the track. Before I started, I wish I'd realized the amount of anxiety OTTBs possess coming off the track. I wish I had been told you cannot layer training over anxiety.

Over five months passed, and I owe it to Denny, along with his barn manager Carrie, for teaching me the importance of patient and slow training that relieves anxiety and builds a strong foundation. ◆

Starting Over: Stories from Re-Riders

COURTNEY PERCIVAL

After years of working for a successful trainer, our relationship soured. I left the barn with shaken confidence and a broken saddle, maybe a few brushes, to start a new journey. It took years before I could purchase my own horse.

After a bit of misfortune-turned-luck, I found a hidden gem of a horse tucked away in the mountains of Montana. She was a trail horse who had become a broodmare. Under her shaggy coat and long mane, I could see the raw talent.

She arrived at my house in the winter of 2010. By 2013, we entered our first recognized show. I was terrified of failure. What would people say about me now? We went out there and won everything that weekend and never looked back. The journey from nothing to success with this horse has been one of the most rewarding experiences of my life. It took leaving a successful barn to really learn the true definition of success and horsemanship. ◆

the hair took a better eye than I had much of the time. But we found some nice young horses.

There is a wedding cake analogy that applies to pricing a horse. A wedding cake has several layers. The backside of a run-down racetrack, at the end of a race meet, is down at that bottom layer, just like the muddy pasture somewhere in East Nowhere, Wyoming. But you buy a horse from places like that, and usually, unless the horse has a soundness or temperament issue that you missed, the young horse has nowhere to go but up.

So, you have a thin, ragged, plain-brown-wrapper four-, five-, or six-year-old off-the-track Thoroughbred gelding, usually barefoot. Now what?

Generally, the first "now what" items are feeding and worming. Teeth floating is up there, as is hoof care. Some are perfectly sound barefoot, some need shoes. Give the horse enough time to fit into a new place before you start the schooling process. "Enough time" might be only a week or two, if the horse is healthy and sound, or it might be six to eight months of pasture

— Pale brown grasslands to the far horizon, dotted in one direction with antelope and the opposite side, by a small band of horses. This was the Blackfeet Reservation in Browning, Montana, where we'd gone to see a mare by our stallion, Right of Light. Talent is where it happens to be. And not always where you might expect to find it. ▲

Years ago, before the proliferation of inexpensive off-track Thoroughbreds (OTTBs), we used to go on Western buying trips. The plain-looking bay mare above, Lynjetter, was in a mountain pasture in Joliet, Montana. In her belly was Just Lyndi, shown in the above right photo with Erin Contino. Running in the field with her sire, Just West, her dam, and others, was the yearling Jetting West, at the top of the page shown with me at Green Mountain Horse Association (GMHA). Some of the youngsters in the field had "stubby" ears, the tips lost to frost bite. Tough environments create either survivors or victims. These were survivors. ▲

rest to clear his system and to let his minor aches and pains go away.

If the horse has been "rode hard and put away wet," the recovery time is apt to reflect this. Try to be patient with him and be sensitive to his situation.

Lots of old-timers use the word "groceries," as in, "What that horse needs is fresh air and groceries." Groceries mean food. It can be green grass, grain, hay, pellets, beet pulp, whatever puts weight on his frame. You've already had his teeth checked, and he is up-to-date on his worming, so unless he has ulcers or some other underlying condition, good food will make him begin to blossom.

The next step is to begin slow work, either in harness or under saddle. Slow means walking. Start with even just half an hour, four or five days a week. Pretty soon, that 30 minutes can get bumped up to 45 minutes, and then to an hour. Once you have him walking out for an hour a day, four, five, or six days a week, you will see some real changes. He's eating well, he's starting to get a base of strength and fitness, the walking is good for his brain, and his coat will start to gleam.

The ugly duckling is beginning to become a swan. It took plenty of management, but the results are starting to show.

That wedding-cake analogy worked because it was a matter of various tiers, and you have changed your horse from the bottom tier to a tier higher on the cake. If you were to price him now for sale, without doing anything else, you have already

increased his appeal. But there are still ways to make that horse step up to the top of the cake, to the place of honor normally reserved for the little bride and groom. These final touches involve showmanship, something that many sellers fail to comprehend. If you bring out this now bright and shiny youngster but he still has a long, scraggly mane, with excess hair on his fetlocks, in an old halter with a rope lead, you are leaving dollars on the table. If the place that you pose the horse is messy and muddy, with a manure spreader and broken fencing in the background, you are leaving more money on the table. If the horse is sloppy and unkempt, that is sending a message too.

Smarten up. Clean the horse, take care of the details, clean his tack, and find a place to present him that reflects the way you want the horse to be perceived. The very same horse presented in one way on one farm can be worth, in the eyes of the buyer, double what he would be worth poorly presented somewhere else.

Actors and actresses do not go to the Oscars dressed like street urchins. If you want a better price for your horse, have him look the part. People are susceptible to appearances, and while appearance isn't everything, never underestimate its power.

— Magic Horses and Just-Fine Horses

Magic sneakers do not exist, but magic horses do. In most sports, all the athletes start out with pretty much the same equipment. Sure, some skis cost more than other skis, and some golf clubs are of better quality than others, but at a high level, all the competitors are even. It isn't as though I have a normal tennis racket and you have one with a ball tracking device that lets your racket make better shots.

This isn't true in sports that involve horses. Secretariat will always beat Dobbin. No horse will outrun the Black Stallion. Magic horses do exist, and if you happen to own one, or a string of them, you are likely to do better than your competition if your riding ability even comes close to theirs. This is the dark little secret about horse sports, hidden in plain sight, and there's not a whole heck of a lot you can do about it except to be born rich, become a business tycoon, win the lottery, or persuade some rich person to sponsor you. You need elite horses to win elite competitions. You need fewer elite horses to win locally, so that's a consolation.

Now there are lots of riders who think that if they need good horses to be able to win, they also need access to good horses in order to become good riders, and that's far less true.

How good a horse do you need in order to learn how to sit the trot? You need a horse that trots. How good a horse do you need in order to develop a feel for an adjustable canter? You need a horse that canters. How good a horse do you need to practice seeing a distance to jump, or to develop a good and effective position over the fence? You need a horse that jumps.

The whole point is that while you do need special horses to have great competitive success, you don't need special horses to become a rider with lots of skills. But you do need access to horses, and this truth stops lots of riders dead in their tracks because they can't figure out how to adjust their lifestyles to coordinate with access to riding horses. Riding practice equals time spent in the saddle, and unless there's a horse under that saddle, it's not such an effective use of your time. ◆ ◆ ◆

BEGIN

a Different Discipline or Activity

My own horse life has had starts and stops and turns and detours, so if there is one thing that I feel qualified to speak about, it is swapping directions by swapping what I've done with horses.

3

_ Starting Over in a Different Type of Riding—or Some Other Horse Involvement

I know a few riders who began in the sport of eventing back in the 1950s and have stuck with just that one sport for 65 or 70 years. Their riding lives would go, if drawn on a map of the United States, like a straight line from Washington, DC, to Los Angeles, California. Those riders didn't deviate, were never tempted to try something new, and are examples of that saying, "He stayed the course."

But many of us have approached things differently.

My own horse life has had starts and stops and turns and detours, so if there is one thing that I feel qualified to speak about, it is swapping directions by swapping what I've done with horses. I made a list of some of the paths I've traveled:

- I started at age 11, riding Western on a pinto pony. I rode in my first gymkhana in 1954, when I was 12.

- Then I rode in my first 100-mile competitive trail ride, also in a Western saddle, at the 1956 GMHA (Green Mountain Horse Association) Trail Ride in Vermont.

— Most breeders are not riders, and most riders are not breeders. For some reason, I was always interested in pedigrees and horse production. I bought my first stallion, Lippitt Raymond here, in 1958, the summer that I would turn 17 years old. He was the first of nearly 20, and the only one with a stud fee of 50 dollars. He also found his way home with me one summer night when I got lost in the dark. Double duty! ▲

- In the fall of 1956, my parents bought me my first Morgan, Lippitt Sandy, and I started showing with an English saddle.

- I bought Lippitt Raymond, a Morgan stallion, in 1958, and started in the breeding business, $50, live foal guaranteed.

- In 1961, while I was working at the Green Mountain Stock Farm, a Morgan show and breeding farm in Randolph, Vermont, I went down to Hamilton, Massachusetts, to watch The Wofford Cup, my first exposure ever to the sport of three-day eventing.

- In the fall of 1961, at Hitching Post Farm in Vermont, not far from where I was a student at Dartmouth College, I got my first jumping and dressage lessons from Joe McLaughlin. I also had my first experience helping to retrain an OTTB (off-the-track Thoroughbred) in the fall of 1961.

- In the spring of 1962, I bought my first Thoroughbred, Lighting Magic, and in July of that year, I competed at my first three-day event.

My eventing phase lasted 50 years, but during that time I had various little side excursions:

Here is Lighting Magic at Hitching Post Farm in South Royalton, Vermont, on the day in May that he was delivered. This was in 1962, and I was in my third year at nearby Dartmouth College. ▲

Starting Over: Stories from Re-Riders

SUSAN ENLOW

I grew up pleasure riding, but after being out of the saddle for 40 years, I found myself at age 60, wishing to be able to sit on a horse again before I got too old to ride.

I connected with a couple who were involved in racing and Thoroughbred farm management and found myself with a wonderful, gentle, beautiful OTTB who had been the "rabbit" in the 2005 Kentucky Derby.

My good fortune was to surround myself with wonderful, knowledgeable horsemen who helped me learn to ride properly and taught me how to manage an athletic horse. Spanish Chestnut (Chet) and I had a blast for nine years, attending sensory training clinics, obstacle courses, natural horsemanship training, dressage lessons, and hacks in the park. ◆

— Raven Sky, a young Thoroughbred stallion standing in Virginia, followed Lippitt Raymond in a long line of stallions I have owned, partially owned, or stood in partnership with others over the last 63 years. I always preferred the stallion end of the breeding business over the mare end. There's less satisfaction, perhaps, but also less potential heartbreak. ▼

— Cold, freezing cold winter jumper shows, where it's 20 degrees Fahrenheit outside, and maybe 10 degrees warmer inside. This was Cat at Old Salem Farm in 1969, and you can see the steam coming from his nostrils. What you can't see are my frozen toes! ▲

- I played polo for a couple of summers.

- I did jumper shows, including one knock-down-and-out class where my horse, Cat, cleared six feet.

- I rode in a couple of point-to-point races, and I hunted for two seasons with the Essex Fox Hounds while I was teaching school in Far Hills, New Jersey.

- Later, as an offshoot of my involvement in three-day eventing, I got involved in sport governance. I was an "Area Chairman" for the US Eventing Association Area 1, and later, I became a member of the USEA Board of Governors. That led to becoming a vice president of the USEA and later president twice during the 1990s.

- I was on the board of the United States Equestrian Team and the American Horse Show Association. I served as president of the Green Mountain Horse Association.

- During my eventing half-century, we stood about 15 sport horse stallions, mostly former stakes-quality Thoroughbred racehorses. I still have part interest in a Thoroughbred stallion, the young Raven Sky.

- I showed in dressage competitions and spent time studying dressage in Germany in the 1980s.

- In the fall of 1997, I added the sport of endurance riding to my list, completing 40 out of 50 rides over about a decade, including seven one-day 100-mile rides. In 2004, I completed the Tevis Cup ride, and have at this point 2,355 competition miles listed in the AERC (American Endurance Ride Conference) records.

- In 2011, I broke my neck in a fall off a horse and decided, at the urging of my doctor, to stop competing in cross-country (I had just turned 70), so I bought a Morgan, High Brook Rockstar, and once again became involved with the Morgan breed. I had always planned to get back into Morgans, I just didn't expect it to take 50 years.

The point here is that each of these paths, or detours, or departures—whatever they might be called—is a clear example of the title of this book. There are thousands of examples. A couple of years ago, we had a young woman from Maine, Kendall Szumilas, here as a summer working student. Right after Kendall graduated from high school, she was looking for an adventure and she found a website for WWOOF (Worldwide Opportunities on Organic Farms). One of the opportunities was a New Zealand breeding farm for endurance Arabians. Kendal applied to be a "WOOFER," got the job, and for over six months got to work with young Arabians, galloped on the beach, and basically enjoyed one of those dream jobs that became reality just because she went for it and made it happen (see p. 160 for more about Kendall's story).

Another working student from just last year, Abby Martin, came to Tamarack Hill Farm, the farm that my wife May and I have owned since 1969, after spending a season running a pack

New Beginnings

Each Day Was a New Beginning for Jane Savoie

By Robert Dover
Olympic Dressage Rider and Author of The Gates to Brilliance

Jane Savoie, who we lost to cancer in January of 2021, was not just my dear friend of over 40 years, she was family. She called my mother "Mom" and my father "Dad," and was happy to get into trouble at events with my sister, Margo. One afternoon in a restaurant in Europe the waiter—noting how similar our hair color and complexions were—asked if she was my "younger sister."

Naturally, Jane loved that (especially the "younger" part) and whenever she would call me after that, she would say, "It's your younger sister...."

Jane's incredible positivity and zest for life were evident in all the new beginnings she undertook, and were an incredibly strong magnet that drew people to her and inspired those who met her to love her. These attributes helped her when she first began in the sport of dressage (I helped her find her first Grand Prix horse, Sacramento) and when she would begin again with new horses or setting new goals that she continually strove to meet, like riding for the Olympic Team (I also helped her find her most successful mount, Zapatero, who was her partner when she was named Reserve Rider for the 1992 Games in Barcelona).

During these last few years, we talked frequently because she knew how strong an advocate I had been for my mother and other family members when they were battling serious health issues. We talked about not settling for answers that were what we did not believe to be the absolute best, and finding the heart to start over with doctors who could give her the latest, cutting-edge therapies. We also spoke about dancing and writing, and the joy she derived from both—things that had once been new challenges that she began and mastered with her usual enthusiasm and will to win.

Jane fought to the end, fueled by her unending spirit and the love and devotion of her wonderful husband and partner in life, Rhett. I know Jane would want us to remember her with all the happiness, excitement, positivity, and joy for new beginnings and second chances that she exuded throughout her life, both professionally and personally. ◆

Denny Emerson | *Begin and Begin Again*

string in the Wind River Range of Wyoming to resupply wilderness campers affiliated with NOLS (National Outdoor Leadership School). Before that job, Abby had been employed to drive carriages on Mackinac Island in Michigan, a place where no mechanized vehicles are permitted. Such adventures do exist, and some of them actually come with a paycheck.

Two of the editors at Trafalgar Square Books, Martha Cook and Rebecca Didier, spent a week at the 400,000-acre Padlock Ranch in Ranchester, Wyoming. Each day they rode out as the cowboys moved cattle from one grazing acre to another, medicated sick cows and followed the daily life of the modern ranch herd. Martha had found out about this through a website called duderanch.org. Once she had a list of possibilities, she asked around for places that were more than walking trail rides, was told about Padlock, and off they went.

Trafalgar Square Managing Director Martha Cook (right) grew up riding and driving Morgans. Managing Editor Rebecca Didier (left) evented. Both New England natives dreamed of spending time on a working ranch out west, and in 2011, they finally made it happen with a week of eight-hour days in the saddle at the Padlock Ranch in Ranchester, Wyoming. ▼

But you don't have to spend money at a dude ranch or travel to New Zealand or Wyoming or Mackinac Island to have an adventure with your horse. You can ride at night under a full moon so bright that your horse casts shadows on the snow, and you can do this in your own backyard. Or you can take your dressage horse on a five-mile walk in the woods. If he has even basic fitness, it won't hurt him, and it will be a departure for both of you if you rarely leave that little sandlot. You can tack up your event horse in a Western saddle and ride at a local dressage show in cowboy dressage or Western dressage. You can teach your Morgan how to drive—get help, if you don't know how—and trot on down some remote dirt road, or do it in the winter in a sleigh, with ringing bells and squeaking snow.

After I had watched the Wofford Cup eventing championship during the summer of 1961, when I was working as an assistant trainer at a Morgan farm in Vermont, I asked the trainer, Art Titus, "Hey, Art! How do I learn how to jump?"

When I got my first pony in 1952, every living person 53 years old or older had been born in the 19th century, and had grown up using horses instead of cars, trucks, and tractors. Getting help learning to harness a horse was easy. So many adults knew how then. Not one in 10,000 does in 2021. ▼

Art replied, "Put up a fence one foot high. Jump it until you get bored. Then raise it."

If you've always wanted to jump, find someone who can teach you the basics, then take the horse you already have, set up some tiny cross-rail jumps about 6 inches high and trot over them. When you get bored, and if your horse is calm about it, raise them.

If you are a Western rider, go ride in an English saddle. If you are an English rider, try a Western saddle. If you are either an English rider or a Western rider, take off the saddle and ride bareback.

See? It doesn't take much to make a change.

_ Learning from Sally Swift

April 28, 1978, Strafford, Vermont. Depending upon the fickle whims of the weather gods, late April in Vermont can feel as warm as mid-May or as wretchedly chilly as mid-March. This particular day was one of those March-like days.

_ When I got Paint in 1952, I was 11. I spent more time bareback than with a saddle for the first couple of years, and it became natural and easy. This past May of 2021, I tried it again on Roxie. Sixty-nine years later, muscle memory kicked in, and it still felt natural. ▲

Sally Swift had driven up to our farm from her home in Brattleboro, Vermont, and had spent the entire day teaching lessons in our indoor ring—not "Centered Riding" lessons as such, because that term had not yet been coined, but lessons that would become the basis of her book *Centered Riding*.

Sally's enthusiasm guaranteed that her lessons would run late, and it wasn't until nearly six in the evening that she drove down to our house with her little Jack Russell Terrier, Joy, to have a cup of tea before heading back down Interstate 91 for the 90-mile drive back to Battleboro.

I can remember this clearly, as if it had happened last week instead of 42 years ago: Sally came into our kitchen with her typical beaming smile.

"What a great way to celebrate my sixty-fifth birthday!"

Think about this. Sixty-five is one of those demarcation dates, when many people retire, move to Florida, or in some way or another begin slowing down. And here was Sally Swift at 65, with most of her towering Centered Riding concept, huge bestselling book, and riding and teaching system still somewhere out in the future, nothing yet written, no system in place.

Sally refused to fall into the trap of equating her age with her potential. Instead of thinking that it was time to hang it up, Sally was just getting started. In 1978, Sally's writing and teaching would continue for almost 30 years, until her death in April 2009.

Her work continues, and *Centered Riding*, published in 1985, is an equestrian bestseller to this day. The book has been translated into 16 languages, and with more than 800,000 copies sold, is the international best-selling horse book of modern times.

_ Rocking Like Walt Gervais

Walt Gervais became something of a celebrity in the American eventing community when he rode in his first long-format Preliminary Level Three-Day Event in Bromont, Quebec, at age 75. Any time I have written about Walt on Facebook, there are comments like, "Well, now I know there's still hope for me."

And yes. Or *maybe*. In order to understand why I am ambivalent about the "still hope for me" sentiment, it's important to understand who Walt Gervais was and to have a better sense of the America in which he came of age. My sense of Walt's history is sort of sketchy, and there may well be gaps and inaccuracies in what I say, but I think the main points will be clear.

Most of us have heard the term "The Greatest Generation," used to describe the Americans who lived through the Great Depression, many of whom served in World War II. Walt was born in 1921, so he was eight years old when the Depression struck in 1929. When Walt was only 14 (I believe his father was no longer around), he had to quit school and get a job to help support his family. Then, when Walt was 20, the

Japanese bombed Pearl Harbor and America got into the war. Walt enlisted in the US Navy and was assigned to the *USS Ranger*, an aircraft carrier that was on convoy duty in the North Sea. (At one point, the *Ranger* was reported by the Germans as sunk by a torpedo, which was not actually the case, but the Navy kept the truth hidden, and for months Walt's family feared he'd been lost at sea.)

Even then, Walt was a good athlete. He entered some sort of Navy boxing tournament and became champion in his weight class.

After the war ended, work was hard to find. Walt was running seriously by then at a sports club in Rhode Island, and he got a job mowing the lawn of the president of a bank in Providence. The bank president looked out of his window one day and saw Walt running up

_ Walt Gervais on the preliminary event course at Groton House—brave, tough, and athletic, totally defying the stereotype that a great-grandfather pushing 80 should be sitting on some porch in some rocking chair. Walt is rocking, all right. But that's no porch, and that's no chair! ▼

The Easiest Place to Start Over

BY STACY WESTFALL

*In 2003, Stacy won her first bridleless freestyle reining competition.
She has since won 12 more—all while riding bridleless.
Twice while bareback and bridleless. In 2006, she was the first woman
to compete in and the first woman to win the Road to the Horse colt-starting
championship. She appeared on* The Ellen DeGeneres Show *in 2008
and gave Ellen a riding lesson. In 2012, Stacy Westfall
was inducted into the Cowgirl Hall of Fame.
Here is a little from Stacy about how it all began.*

– DENNY EMERSON –

Often the easiest place to start over is from rock bottom. That is not to say that I recommend steering your life toward rock bottom as your chosen starting point, but knowing it can be a starting point can be useful information if you should find yourself there.

I found myself at rock bottom in 2003.

On the surface, it looked like I had everything I wanted. And, on paper, I literally had everything I wanted. Five years earlier, my husband had arrived home to find his wife holding their small child and excitedly waving a paper at him. "Here, I made two of these papers, I'm going to write down what I want to achieve in the next five years. Will you do the same?" He did.

Five years later I had check marks next to everything on the five-year list and most of the things on the 10-year list: house; barn and indoor arena; training horses full time, and so on. I had it all. And I cried myself to sleep every night.

My husband was concerned but also confused. (What does she want? Maybe it's just her hormones...she has had three kids in the last four years. It must be that.)

I was no help. Aside from crying and reporting I was miserable, I was unable to find the words to express my deeper feelings. I just knew something was missing.

Finally, one night I blurted out something like, "I just hate training horses like this! It's like I'm training robots! It's nothing like I imagined it would be. I would rather get rid of it all, go back to work at McDonald's and own one horse I love than to do this!"

Even if it didn't make sense to anyone else (especially my poor bombarded husband), at least I had finally found what was missing: relationship.

I'd grown up with two equines before going off to college—my pony from age six and then my

— Stacy Westfall could sit on an aardvark and make it look good. A couple of years ago she stopped in at our farm in Vermont, showed us some of her horses, and rode my Thoroughbred, Tense. Here are several photos from her visit. These naturally gifted riders can just do it. She jumped Tense, and it looked like that's all she did with horses instead of something she almost never does.... ▲

| 3 | Begin a Different Discipline or Activity

first horse from age 12, both of whom were still living at the time of my meltdown—and relationship wasn't ever in question. It was the obvious but unspoken reason for owning them.

Somewhere between "Equine Nutrition 101" and "Horse Training 402," my equine college professors had failed to point out that relationship wasn't part of the deal. Granted, the term "natural horsemanship" wasn't popular at the time,

— Stacy riding my OTTB, Tense. ▲

but even today, when I look into many areas of the competitive horse world, the importance of relationship is often missing from the equation.

Having a revelation is one thing. Taking action on it is another. I repeated my "I'd rather go back to McDonald's" statements many more times before I realized the full implications. I could feel the pull of wanting something different, but also the truth that McDonald's might not be the direction that would take me there.

It finally occurred to me that if I really was okay giving it all up, I could make choices that had previously seemed too risky.

I began looking at the horses, the customers, and my business through a completely different lens. The horses responded immediately to my more open and playful approach. Where before I had been concerned about winning at the

next show to keep the customers happy and paying the bills, now I was more focused on bringing out the best in my horses, which might or might not lead to winning at the next show.

I also began talking to my customers about these things more openly. Whereas before I was worried about making the customers happy, I was now more concerned with explaining my choices—and letting them make their choices.

All the while, I was honoring my relationships with the horses as I trained them.

And if all the customers left and we couldn't pay the bills, off to McDonald's I would go. Spoiler alert: the customers didn't leave, and I didn't go off to McDonald's.

Instead, this newfound direction, this willingness to let go of everything I had and everything I thought I had ever wanted, gave me the freedom to make decisions that year that would set me on a path to achieve more than I had ever dared to dream.

I hope you never find yourself at rock bottom, but if you do, then between sobs, take a look up. If you're somewhere you don't want to be, what's the harm in trying something new? ◆

the steep lawn, pushing the mower. He went out and asked Walt whether he was being paid by the job or by the hour.

"By the hour," said Walt.

"Well," said the banker, "you don't need to kill yourself."

"That's okay," said Walt. "I run anyway," as off he went, simultaneously running and mowing.

The bank president was so impressed that he hired Walt on the spot to do maintenance work at the bank, a job Walt kept for decades. In his many years of working at the multistory bank tower, Walt had made sure to walk up all the flights of stairs at least three times every day, "two steps at a time," he told me.

In 1946, Walt finished twenty-fifth in the Boston Marathon. The next year, Walt was running in fourth place in the Marathon, with only six miles to go, when his knee blew out.

When Walt, whose wife had died, was somewhere in his mid-fifties, he heard that one of the best places to meet pretty women was at horseback riding stables, so he started taking lessons.

He was a serious competitor in every sport he took up, and I first met him when I was teaching a riding clinic in Rhode Island. Walt had by that time retired from his work at the bank and he asked me if he and I could make a deal. "I want to get better," said Walt, "and you need someone to do maintenance at your farm."

Walt's horse was a somewhat flighty OTTB—a pretty chestnut gelding, green about dressage and not always the bravest horse in cross-country. But Walt was determined, and he began to get clean rounds at the Novice Level. When he was 69, he won his first Novice event at Huntington Farm in Vermont.

Shortly after that came a big opportunity that totally changed the trajectory of Walt's riding career.

David O'Brian, a working student at Tamarack Hill Farm, had been competing at the Advanced level with a big, bay gelding named Sail On Simcoe. The gelding, nicknamed "Timmy," was coming to the end of his upper-level days of competing, and since David and Walt were good friends, David asked Walt if he would like to ride Timmy.

So now Walt was 72, Timmy was around 14 or 15, I think, and they began to forge a new partnership. That summer, the Area One USEA Eventing Championships were being hosted at Huntington Farm, just a couple of miles up the road from us. Walt and David and I had been toying with the idea of having this be Walt's first Preliminary attempt, so David walked the cross-country course.

"It's a true championship-level course," David told me. "Plenty big, but Timmy can do big. I'm going to tell Walt that it's a go. No need to tell him how hard it is!"

So Walt's first clean round was over the hardest course in Area One.

Three years later, Walt was 75 and had yet to ride in a full three-day, with longer distances and higher speeds. Bromont, Quebec, about three hours north of us, was going to host a three-day using some of the same courses that had been in the 1976 Olympics. Walt entered the event.

One evening, about a week before the event, I saw Walt grazing Timmy on the lawn behind the barn. "So how's it going?" I asked.

"Joyce doesn't want me to do it," said Walt, who had, by now, remarried. "My kids, they don't want me to do it. My grandkids, they don't want me to do it. They even got my little great grandson to say, 'Grampy, don't do it.'"

"Wow, Walt," I responded. "Those are all your family who love you and care about you. What do you say to them when they tell you that?"

Walt's colorful reply cannot be printed in this book.

So Walt rode Timmy at Bromont, and for several years after that. One hot summer day, when Walt was in his early eighties, I saw him loading big hay bales into the tractor bucket to haul around and drop off at the two other barns.

I said something like, "Hot day for all of that, Walt." I've never forgotten his reply.

"You know, I don't particularly *enjoy* doing this. I don't think it's fun. But I know I am doing myself some good."

A couple of years later, one sunny evening, when Walt was beginning to feel the effects of a lung disease that would eventually end his life, I saw him sitting in a folding chair by the pond.

"Well, finally," I thought to myself. "Walt is at last able to sit and relax and watch the sunset."

When I got closer, I saw that he had an iron dumbbell in each hand. He was doing a series of curls.

So, yes—or maybe—there's hope for all of us, as can be seen in the Walt Gervais story. Walt was one of those old Viking warriors, brave and tough and gritty, brought up in a tough and gritty era in our country's history.

When I find myself getting wimpy, if I remember to think, "What would Walt do?" I can usually keep pushing a little more tenaciously. But he's a hard act to follow.

_ Coming Back to Riding

Some years ago, the Dutch dressage champion Anky van Grunsven wrote about the difference between big and little transitions in dressage. A "big" transition might be to bring a horse from a canter to a halt. A "little" transition would be a walk to a halt.

It's the same with new beginnings. Changing from one discipline to another, say from riding saddle seat to riding show hunters, is a "bigger" new beginning than changing riding instructors within the same style of riding.

Coming back into riding after 10 years away is a *bigger* new beginning than coming back into riding after, say, a six-month military deployment.

Starting to ride again after healing from a broken collar bone is a much *smaller* new beginning than coming back from a double mastectomy.

Typically, the smaller the new beginning, the easier, which is not to say that "little" new beginnings can't be significant.

_ When a horse and rider "warm up," they literally do, through increased blood flow. That warmth translates into greater flexibility and range of motion, and it decreases the chances of strains and tears. Here, Sue Berrill and Phoebe are warming up for cross-country at an event at the GMHA—a cool morning, sun filtering through the rising mist. ▼

NEDA (New England Dressage Association) hosts a major trainer every fall to give a three-day seminar, and about eight years ago I went to UMass, Amherst, to observe the Klaus Balkenhol clinic. If you don't know about Klaus, he was a German Olympian and World Champion, as well as coach of the bronze-medal-winning US Dressage Team in 2004. As each group at the clinic began, Klaus emphasized the key importance of a minimum of 10 minutes of walking, an active but not hurried walk, as a sort of interlude between not working and working. He said to look at your watch, because 10 minutes can feel like 20 if you've typically taken much less time.

He said that riders who get on and walk once or twice around the arena, pick up the reins, and start to trot, haven't let their horse fully adjust to the situation. The horse might be stiff, might hurry, might put his head in the air. The rider might react to the tension in the horse by getting tight with her arms, and before things have even started they are already going badly.

"People want to get through the warmup so they can get to the real work. The warmup *is* real work," he'd say.

This changed my perspective entirely. I went home and never did a too-fast warm up ever again. It was a "little" new beginning with big consequences. Any new beginning brings with it new chances for becoming better, staying the same, or getting worse. We can choose one of these if we are aware that the choice exists. Becoming more aware is a new beginning in its own right.

_ "Re-Riders": The Biggest New Beginning

There's no fixed time frame for how long someone has to be out of riding before coming back to be considered a card-carrying "re-rider," but it probably needs to be measured in years, if not decades.

Stephen Day used to be the owner of Stateline Track and then of Dover Saddlery, so he had his finger very directly on the pulse of who rides and who does not.

I asked him, "Steve, who are your customers?"

His immediate reply: "Teenage girls and their mothers."

If you think this through, there's a big gap between a 16- or 17-year-old girl and that same woman enough years later to have a teenager of her own. How long a gap? Well, figure it out. Let's assume that the rider was at least in her early twenties before she had a child. So, say she was 25, and in modern times, this may be a bit early, on average. But say 25, just as a starter.

Now add 13, because that's the first teenage year. So, for the mother to be able to even have a teenage child, she's probably going to be in her forties. Let's assume that this now 40-something mother was a horse-obsessed child back when she was being supported by her parents. But then along came college, or employment, and her parents dropped her off the dole. She may have moved into a city where she could get a better job. No horse there. She may have gotten married, done what so many newly married couples do, struggled to make the finances work. No horse there. Then she and her husband started a family. More financial struggle, years of childcare, being an unpaid chauffeur...no horse there.

But now our hypothetical former teenage rider is perhaps 45 or so, maybe a little younger or a bit older, and she finds that the money isn't as tight. She might have a better job. She might not be spending as much time ferrying kids around. And the bug hasn't gone away. That horse desire has been lying there dormant all these years, not extinguished, but asleep, like a hibernating bear in winter.

— What Wakes the Sleeping Bear?

Who knows just what wakes the sleeping bear? Maybe she has a friend who has a horse. Maybe her daughter is taking lessons at a stable. Maybe the family has moved to a suburb farther from town or city, and closer to rural places where there are barns and stables.

Starting Over: Stories from Re-Riders

CHRISTEN SCHWEIZER

As a poor preteen, I devoured horse books. My biggest dream was to own tall boots and a horse. Showing was unattainably expensive. Obsessed with detail, I would saw out the mouths of my Breyer horses to be able to put paperclip bits properly in their mouths.

I eventually worked at a nearby barn in exchange for riding. I was amazingly given horses to ride and worked at other barns, but I never owned tall boots or showed.

Horses faded from my life, but I have brought them back with a vengeance. Today I have two horses in our gorgeous backyard. My daughter and I have been to schooling shows. And I still get a thrill when I zip up my very own real tall boots. ◆

... What is "equitation?" Right down there, at the level of the very roots of the word, the term, the concept, would be this simple definition: "Equitation is the blending of two bodies, that of the horse and that of the human, so harmoniously that, like the mythical Centaur, they become one creature, one entity." This is so often a lifelong quest, beginning with the acquisition of an independent seat, as this young woman being longed is attempting to achieve. ▼

I got this email not long ago:

I was hoping you could provide some input regarding equitation. I know as an eventer it is not a class you would have much personal experience with but, after listening to a pro Jumper rider provide his opinion on equitation, I realized that the definition of "equitation" is a bit ambiguous.

I always understood it to apply to any and all disciplines as having good mechanics such as a stable seat, good use of aids, control of the horse and, to some level, finesse. I tried to find the definition of "equitation" on the USHJA and USEF sites but found nothing of substance.

Any insight to what the origins of equitation were, and how they have morphed, would be great. Thank you for your time.

If you look in the dictionary, equitation is defined as "the art or practice of riding horses," which doesn't tell us much that we didn't already know.

Any time that a human climbs on a horse and asks the horse to do just about anything, the presence of that rider will be a hindrance to the horse, in the sense that the horse performs athletic feats more easily if unencumbered by weight on his back.

So, following this path of logic: "good" equitation must involve the art of riding the horse in a manner that, while giving signals and aids, creates the least disruption and the least encumbrance, allowing the horse his best chance of performing the task at hand.

Which leads to words like balance, centeredness, harmony, softness, agility, elasticity, all conveying that the human is staying in the best possible position, changing constantly as the horse moves, to permit the horse to do his job.

And this should hold true for all types of riding, at all gaits, on all terrain, in all sorts of saddles, in every kind of action.

Functional equitation, therefore, is "stylized" most correctly if the style being displayed gets the rider as completely as possible out of the way of the horse, because it is primarily the horse that has to function.

When "equitation" becomes stiff, falsely stylized, something done for its own sake rather than for the sake of the horse's ability to perform, it can't be called good equitation. ◆

She might have watched *Secretariat* on Netflix, or perhaps she got a subscription to *The American Quarter Horse Journal* or the *The Morgan Horse Magazine*.

Whatever the stimulus happens to be, and however long the hiatus may have been, she is entering the chrysalis stage in the life cycle of a butterfly. A metamorphosis is taking place, leading to the giant step of putting a foot into the stirrup of a saddle strapped to the back of an actual horse, swinging her leg over, and feeling again, after so many years, what her body and soul have never forgotten—what it means to ride a horse.

This rebirth may come easily, or it can be laden with anxiety, trepidation, even real fear. The physical body after 10, 20, 30 or more years is probably not the body she had in high school. While the kid rode with the confidence and easy courage of someone who'd never been hurt, the adult version of that young Valkyrie is all too aware of mortality. She has the dubious privilege of a more fully developed brain that is able to relate present action to future consequence. She's probably more risk aware because of all this, and the experience that her new self seeks won't be the same as the experiences that she remembers. Maybe later, as she gets back in shape and more in tune, but first things first.

There's an old saying about how once you learn to ride a bike, you always know how to ride a bike. It's sort of the same way with riding a horse, but a bike, being an inanimate object, can be relied upon to perform in accordance with how it is handled in a mechanical formula. Certain pressures here in the pedals and handles lead to certain actions there. Not so with a living, breathing horse. Some horses are predictable and straightforward in their responses; others are that way much of the time, except perhaps on a frosty fall morning when they are feeling feisty—but there are some horses that are ticking time bombs. It is so important to ride the right horse.

When you first started riding all those years ago on a horse that gave you confidence, success built upon success—remember that? So be even more sure about getting on a horse that will make you feel good this time around. Of course, there are some who are fit and tough and brave and athletic at any age, but unless you are one of that small band of warrior athletes, you are much better off to start "easy" and see where it goes than to just climb aboard some half-broke, nervous horse that is probably just as unsure about you as you are about him.

The main challenge will be to find the Steady Eddie that lets you start over. I keep coming back to my former USET coach Jack Le Goff's saying about how a horse or a rider develops courage: "Boldness comes from confidence. Confidence comes from success. It, therefore, becomes the goal of trainers to create many situations that pretty much guarantee success."

As the re-rider gets back into relearning what it feels like to walk, trot, canter, and maybe, to start jumping, one giant variable will be how often she gets to ride. Are you in a position to dive back in, by possibly buying a horse and riding several times or more each week, or are you one who first dips a toe in the water, then a foot, then a knee?

If you are easing your way back, one of the time-honored methods is to take a lesson or two each week at some local riding school. If it's a well-run barn with a competent staff of teachers, the trainer will match you with the right horses. I have two friends who are doing this. Ted is in his late seventies and Judy is in her early eighties, and they both ride together once a week at a local barn on horses owned by the farm. This arrangement gives both of my friends their riding fix, it doesn't cost them much, and they are free of all the obligations that go along with owning the horses. It works for them.

Someone else might want more, and there are options short of full horse ownership, such as half leases, where two people share the expense of one horse and ride different days. I know of one woman who has a deal with a local stable that she can exercise a couple of the school horses in exchange for working Saturday and Sunday mornings, feeding and cleaning stalls.

There are all sorts of strategies and arrangements. Look around, ask around. Try to find a situation that works for you.

— Ted Niboli, Judy Cameron Baswood, and I have been friends since the mid-1950s. We met because of our mutual interest in Morgan horses, we showed together decades ago, and we are still riding together 65 years later. ▲ ▶

_ The Girl in the Mural

There are "Road to Damascus" life-altering reversals of direction changes, and there are tiny ones. This is true in everything, of course, not just in matters pertaining to riding.

Looking back 60 years, I am pretty sure that my most life-altering change happened when I was a freshman at Dartmouth College. Either in the fall of 1959, or in the winter of 1960, I got my midterm grades and saw that I was failing a required freshman science class.

For all my life I had been one of those students who found that anything that required reading or writing was easy, but those subjects that required study and memorization of facts or concepts were not easy. For some reason, and later it seemed ridiculous to me that I didn't grasp it, I thought that if I could not instantly totally comprehend some body of knowledge, I couldn't do it. In Latin, for example, you obviously had to simply memorize what the various words meant. I didn't memorize them. In math, you had to learn that seven times nine equals 63; I didn't understand the necessity of memorizing multiplication tables. In chemistry, there were all sorts of things that had to be learned. I didn't learn them.

It was partly—mostly—my own fault that I got good grades in English, history, any written subject, and failing or mediocre grades in the subjects that required study.

No single teacher ever sat me down and explained to me that I didn't know how to study. They told me that I was capable of doing well, but none even said, "You have to *memorize*, you have to *study*." I just didn't get it. Why I didn't remains a mystery. It should have been obvious, but all I can say is that, to me, it was not obvious.

I went to superior schools, Bement for eighth grade, and Phillips (Andover) Academy for the first three years of high school, getting As in my easy subjects, C-, Ds, and Fs in my "bad" subjects. Finally, after my third year of Andover saw me failing math and chemistry, I got "fired," as they euphemistically called it. "Flunked out" was the real way to say it. My parents scrambled to find another school, and I spent my senior year at Vermont Academy in Saxtons River, Vermont.

In terms of nurture, VA was a far different place than PA. Andover in the 1950s was one of those sink-or-swim places, with little sympathy for those who didn't get it done. The faculty at Vermont Academy were far more available, and I had a reasonably successful senior year. With good grades that last high school year, good recommendations, and good SAT results, plus a strong family history of Dartmouth uncles, father, and great-grandfather, I got admitted to Dartmouth, and yet here I was once again, looking at a failing grade in science.

I do not to this day completely understand what triggered my reversal of course, but I think that I had finally had it with doing poorly in school. I had done all of what little studying I did in my dorm room in Fayerweather Hall. Somehow, I realized that if I tried to study there, I'd have a million distractions and I would succumb to all of them. I remember picking up a stack of books and walking over to the Orozco Mural Room at Baker Library, where there were rows and rows of long tables and chairs. Everyone there was studying. There was no other purpose for being there.

I sat down in a chair. I opened a book, and for the first time in my life, at the age of 18, I actually began to study. The room where I studied had floor-to-ceiling murals by the Mexican artist José Clemente Orozco along the side walls, and one of the scenes was of a teacher and her little pupils. One small girl had a somber face and a jutting jaw, which made her look stubbornly resolute. It was resolution I had lacked, so I made her into a sort of role model.

I pulled my failing grade to a C-, and for the next four years I never looked back. When I graduated with distinction in my major field of English in 1963, I was one of the only two in that big major to do so.

Being smart enough was nowhere near good enough. I had to add a stubborn determination to do the work. Where that lightning bolt came from—the realization that I had to make a huge change, and that the change was going to be hard—I still don't know. The thing is, I did it. And the ramifications of that turnaround had lasting effects, which had little to do with academics. For once I had discovered that it was within me to decide upon a goal and work to reach it. I could use that power in lots of other ways. ◈ ◈ ◆

BEGIN

Facing Down Your Fears

If you are a "newbie," don't be afraid of being nervous, because that anxiety is totally normal. Usually, as you "get your feet wet," to use that familiar saying, you'll find that nervousness ebbing.

_ Fear of Beginning

There are many causes of fear in riding, and some of them have more to do with a previous injury or experience, while others are bound up with a particular horse.

_ "Newbies"

If you are a "newbie," don't be afraid of being nervous, because that anxiety is totally normal. Usually, as you "get your feet wet," to use that familiar saying, you'll find that nervousness ebbing.

It isn't unusual to be nervous about an activity that is unfamiliar. An avid sailor might feel totally at ease on a boat but be riddled with anxiety about driving an 18-wheeler in traffic. The truck driver who lives behind a wheel might be calm in a snowstorm while navigating the George Washington Bridge in rush hour but paralyzed with fear to be standing on rented skis at the top of a Vermont mountain slope. Beginning riders are often insecure and anxious for the same reasons

Starting Over: Stories from Re-Riders

Sophia von Hofacker

I dreamed of riding my whole childhood. I was not allowed. That dream came back with a vengeance when I was about to turn 49 and we visited my brother-in-law who owned Friesians. I decided I had to learn to ride. NOW.

At first I was afraid of everything—not on the ground, but in the saddle. And I am a slow learner, and I ended up having a ton of bad trainers. But now, almost a decade and three great trainers later I have: jumped; ridden bareback; cantered a Barb gelding and an Arab stallion on the beaches and through olive groves in Tunisia; hacked a nervous mare in Greece who went backward more than half the time; ridden in groups in Austria; survived four falls (two of those from a Lipizzaner and one fit to take me out—it was pure luck my head was still on my spine when I got up from the dust to finish our quadrille); started to treat my clients (I am a trauma therapist) with equine help, which is a dream come true that I hadn't realized I even had.

And the best? In February 2020, I bought my own horse. A mare with a mind of her own, a seasoned partner that I can learn from and grow with—and just generally, I am having the time of my life! ◆

as the sailor in traffic or the truck driver on skis. They are not in their element, and they won't be until enough time has been spent doing the new thing.

I live next door to Fort Bragg in the winter, and I know quite a few Special Forces soldiers. Now those guys are about as brave and tough as anyone, anywhere, any time, but even *they* have told me that it was lots harder to make that first jump out of an airplane than their fifty-first, and so on.

— Re-Riders

We've already talked a little about re-riders (see p. 54). If you have been away from riding for years and are coming back to it as an adult, it can be like being a green beginner all over again. Sure, someone might tell you that it's like riding a bike, or swimming—things that, once you have learned them, will come automatically back to you as muscle memory. What they don't tell you, though, as I've already pointed out, is that a living, breathing horse isn't the same thing as a bicycle. Just because you stop, the horse doesn't necessarily stop.

Your life circumstances as a 43-year-old re-rider are totally unlike what they were when you stopped riding at 23. Your body may be quite different. Your obligations to others are greater. You have more to lose.

So, again, if you are starting again, treat it the same way you did back all those years

ago when you were first green. Try not to blame or shame yourself if you feel nervous. Take your time. Baby steps. You'll be fine if you give yourself enough time.

_ Illness or Injury

There are two other related reasons for feeling trepidation: coming back to riding after a serious illness, or coming back after a serious injury, perhaps one that did not involve horses. In both cases, you will likely feel weak and unfit, and the best advice I have heard about this is simple. Don't push it. Take your time. Ride an easy, quiet horse. Walk. Stay in a confined space.

You are doing this for you, not for them, whoever "they" might be. Take all the time you need. If you don't want to jump again, don't. If you don't want to canter again, don't. If you don't want to trot, don't trot. Do what *you* want. It is your recovery.

You may come back eventually to as good as new, or you might not. Cross that bridge when you come to it. For now, though, take it one step at a time.

Now if it so happens that you are returning to riding after a bad horse-related accident, you may be facing a double whammy. You are as weak physically as those who were sick or injured, but you may also be playing that accident over and over in an endless spool in your mind. So, this is tougher, no doubt about it.

If you fell off because your horse slipped and fell on ice, you can "feel" that. If he spun out from under you, your toes clench, waiting for the spin. If he bucked you off or bolted, you imagine a repeat move on his part.

So, what to do? Number one: DO NOT START BACK ON THE HORSE THAT HURT YOU. You maybe can ride that one again later, but get your confidence back first, preferably on a horse that doesn't do what that one did.

Again, baby steps. See where they lead. Again, it is your recovery.

There are mind-related fears that are far outside my understanding, and I would no more try to address these than I would try to help someone who asked me to set his broken leg.

Starting Over: Stories from Re-Riders

ASHLEY CRIHFIELD

I was a former Preliminary event rider, now empty-nester, who had not owned a horse for 35 years. I bought a four-year-old Arabian gelding in an online auction because I was eager to rekindle my passion for horses and pursue a new discipline—competitive trail riding. Six months later, the horse reared while I was mounting, and I fell and badly broke both wrists.

After a difficult recovery, including oxycontin addiction, I pushed through intense fear and anxiety when I got back on my highly reactive but talented horse and headed out on the trails of Vermont. Mile by mile, day by day, year after year, my horse and I gained each other's trust. Now, five years later, we have successfully completed every distance ride we've entered, including the 2018 GMHA 100 Mile, and won many. Now focused on dressage, we are currently showing Second Level. ◆

Some anxieties and fears need professional help, and I am no such professional. I hope you will seek those sources, if these simple ideas don't work.

_ Why Does This Horse Scare Me?

I don't know any rider who likes to be afraid when she rides. Riders who love to ride are almost never scared to ride. If your goal is to be a happy rider, you need to figure out how to avoid situations that make you nervous. It seems pretty obvious, right? I mean, who loves to ride scared?

But in real life, too many people do ride scared, and in most of these cases, the reason they are white-knuckled is because of one, two, or three basic reasons: 1) They are riding a horse that scares them, or 2) they are riding at a level that is beyond their comfort zone, or 3) they are riding a horse that scares them at a level that is beyond their comfort zone.

Think this through by working backward. You are riding a horse who doesn't scare you, and you are riding this horse in a situation and style and manner that is within your comfort zone. Are you scared? Probably not.

My Facebook page has over 100,000 "followers." One day I asked the question, "What is it that horses do that cause you anxiety?" I got hundreds of responses. According to the feedback I received, here are some of the most normal causes of fear:

- Horses that rear.

- Horses that buck.

- Horses that spook and spin.

- Horses that bolt.

_ Rearing isn't as dangerous as bucking, unless the horse falls over backward onto the rider. But because that can sometimes happen, although rarely, I think it should be avoided. And the best way to avoid being reared with is simple. If it rears, don't ride it! ◄

- Horses that trip and fall down.

- Horses that are reactive while being mounted.

- Horses that slam you around while they are being handled on the ground.

There are a few more, but that's a pretty big list. Let's discuss them.

_ Rearing

If I were to pick just one cause of fear to avoid, rearing would be it. When someone says, "That horse is a rearer," it means that the horse has almost a button or switch, and any time the horse feels pressure, the switch gets flipped, and up he goes. This is different from what you might call a little "worry hop."

The rearing by itself is less dangerous than what can happen when the horse rears so high that he loses his balance and topples over backward and lands on his rider. I have two friends who are trainers, and both of them had former students who were killed by horses that reared and fell over backward on top of them. Half a ton slamming down on a human from a height of six or seven feet in the air is lethal. In addition to the two dead riders, I have heard of many other deaths and truly horrific injuries caused by a rearing horse.

Rearing becomes the automatic response that the horse does in all kinds of situations: when he's being asked to leave the barn, perhaps, to pass through a muddy place on a trail, or when his friend heads off in a different direction. The horse responds to his anxiety by going up. And up.

There is one simple solution: DO NOT RIDE A HORSE THAT REARS.

_ Bucking

Bucking can be something that a playful horse might do out of exuberance, or it might be what the bucking horses at rodeos do: buck to get the rider off. So, in some ways, there are "real buckers," and there are horses that might throw in a buck. Between these extremes are anxious horses who "go to bucking" in some circumstances but seem pretty safe "most of the time."

So, what is *your* tolerance level? Probably, unless you are a rodeo cowboy, you will avoid the real buckers. Why wouldn't you? Do you *like* trips to the emergency room?

For the exuberant, playful bucks, maybe crow-hops on a chilly morning, there can be strategies to alleviate this behavior. One is to longe the horse before riding him. An old-time hunter trainer named Ronnie Mutch had two sayings about longeing high-spirited horses. One was, "I think of my longe line as a 20-foot-long tranquilizing needle." The other: "Better 10 minutes with a longe line than 10 weeks in a cast."

But you need to decide if it is worth the risk. In many ways, the horse who seems placid enough but who can suddenly explode into bucking is the most dangerous, because you don't know if or when it is going to happen.

My advice to riders who really and truly don't want to run the risk of getting hurt is to think of both rearers and buckers as horses to avoid. There's a saying about this: "They can't buck you off if you're not on!"

Spookers and Spinners

We've all had it happen. It is a sunny summer afternoon, and we are heading home after a relaxing ride on the trails. The horse is swinging along, head down, relaxed and happy. You have loose reins, relaxed and happy.

A doe, sleeping in the bush beside the trail, leaps and bolts. One second your horse is heading east. A nanosecond later, he is heading west. If you are still on top, it's a miracle.

Even the calmest horses have triggers. Anything sudden, unexpected, quick, and loud can pull that trigger, so I don't know if there exists any foolproof method to avoid the spook and spin.

That said, some horses are much spookier than others.

There was a logger named Eddie Nelson who used a Belgian draft horse named Admiral to haul logs from where Eddie felled the tree back to the log landing. I watched Admiral stand there, untethered, while Eddie ran a snarling chainsaw at the base of a big maple. Admiral didn't blink when the tree crashed to the ground. Eddie limbed the log, backed Admiral to one end, wrapped a chain around the log, and chirped to Admiral, who trudged off, dragging it to the landing.

A horse like Admiral has a low spook response. Others will flinch when a mouse burps. Pick your level of tolerable spook. One method, when you ride in company, is to have the least reactive horse go in front. Some spooky horses will follow where they won't lead. There is no one-size-fits-all answer.

_ Bolters and Runaways

Terrifying. When a horse bolts, he loses his mind. He can run into traffic, off a ledge, or into a barbed wire fence. If I owned a bolter, I would send him to someone who deals with these sorts of issues, and if he couldn't fix it, I would get rid of the horse. Bolters that remain bolters are as dangerous as rearers and buckers.

_ Trippers and Stumblers

I've watched Arabian endurance horses trot and even canter on loose reins down rock-strewn slopes where a cat might fear to tread. I've watched horses trip and fall on fields as smooth and manicured as a putting green at the US Open.

Some horses have self-carriage and an instinct for self-preservation that others lack. This is simple reality. But there are a few strategies that help keep horses upright, and being aware of footing is one of them.

Ice is treacherous, and funnily enough, slick mowed grass on a dry slope can be almost as slippery as ice. Downhill causes more tripping than uphill. A trip at a walk is less likely to cause a horse to fall than a trip at a faster gait. Good shoeing can help. Not letting a horse go half asleep can help. Riding with vigilance can be better than slouching along with long reins.

I read about some old cowboy who rode out in the mountains. He was asked what he did about horses that stumbled. He said something like this: "If they stumble once, they get another chance, but the second time they stumble, I get rid of them."

That's pretty extreme, but it's one solution.

_ Mounting (and Dismounting) Issues

Unless a horse has other underlying panic issues, he can usually be taught to stand like a rock while you are getting on and getting off, but if you don't know how to train this into a horse, get help from someone who does know.

Much of the problem can simply be because we fail to insist every single time that the horse stand still and not move off until he is asked. Whether you get on from the ground, from a mounting block, or from some impromptu version of a mounting block such as a stump, an inclined bank, or a rock, the horse should learn to wait until you give him the signal to move away.

You can't do this some of the time and expect him to understand. You have to do this *all* the time, every time. And the same with dismounting. Stand like a stone, do not move a single inch. Build that behavior into the horse through calm consistency.

— Getting Pushed Around

Horses need to learn ground manners. They have to be taught to respect human boundaries. They need to be taught to lead quietly, to cross-tie, to tie to a trailer, to load, to back up, to move away, to come forward.

They need to learn not to bite and kick. Horses need boundaries, and most horses can learn boundaries. If you do not know how to teach manners, find someone who does or be forever pushed around by your untrained horse.

— It's Supposed to Be Fun

Finding the "why" in why you're afraid is the start of the cure. You can't fix it when you don't know what's causing it. And it can be a Sherlock Holmes mystery, or it can be as simple as having a horse that bucks when you shouldn't ride a horse that bucks.

If you are not sure why you are afraid, if that fear is consuming and it sucks the joy out of your relationship with horses, don't be afraid to seek professional help, whether from horse people or from professional counselors who know about dealing with anxiety issues. Riding, driving, and being around horses is supposed to be fun. If fear, anxiety, and dread make it otherwise, doesn't it make sense to face it squarely, and to try to fix it?

— Fear and Training

Now let's consider fear in the horse.

Can you study in any productive way when you have a headache? Not such an ideal learning situation, don't you think? Why should a horse who is nervous, fearful, uncomfortable, or in actual pain be any different?

Here is some horse with a leverage sort of bit, a cranked-tight cavesson, being made to perform canter-to-walk transitions by a hard-handed rider who is wearing spurs and carrying a dressage whip. When the horse doesn't come back readily, he gets jabbed in the mouth. If he doesn't quickly pick up the correct lead, he gets spurred and smacked with the whip.

Is this horse in a good learning place? Is this horse receptive to the aids? Is this horse supple and elastic? Are the lessons being forced upon him lessons that will create a more supple, willing, and calmly responsive horse?

Can a horse who is tense and fearful and in discomfort learn, or is the first job of the rider, before any training is possible, to try to get the horse to be calm and comfortable? Again I ask: Do you learn better when you are being scared and bullied? If you don't learn that way, why might you think that it's somehow different for your horse?

_ Word to the wise: when you are leading something that weighs 3,000 pounds and has steel shoes, do not wear flip-flops. ▲

_ "Good riders don't bounce." Have you ever watched some rider bouncing along at the sitting trot, and thought to yourself, "What a good rider!" No? Neither have I. Practice more, yearn less, for more chances of successfully dealing with those shock waves produced by the movement of the horse's swinging back, so that you can absorb them rather than be slammed around by them. I learned to sit the trot by riding bareback. ▷

In nearly all training situations, most horses, most of the time, are less than perfect. How often, in real life, do we experience anything like the ideal ride? It's partly because we don't find that lovely harmony, that partnership, that makes training necessary in the first place. In other words, during training, it is not unusual to think, "This horse is not doing what I want," or to think, "This horse is not performing the way that I'd like."

So here comes the fork in the road. The not-so-good trainer is apt to think, "This horse won't do what I want. Therefore, this horse is being bad," or "He is disobedient," or some similarly negative word. The moment this conclusion gets reached, the rider-trainer gives herself permission to punish the bad behavior.

The good trainer may also feel, "This horse is not doing what I want." But the good trainer now thinks, "Why is this happening? Is my horse uncomfortable? Is the saddle fitting poorly? Is the cavesson or girth too tight? Could he have ulcers? Is my seat too unsteady? Are my hands not sympathetic enough?"

Denny Emerson | _Begin and Begin Again_

Field Notes
Age and Training

Most of the better horsemen and horsewomen that I know are great believers in the "let horses be horses" theory of horse management. Let them buck and play and race and spin, even knowing that, yes, they CAN get hurt. It's better than putting them into a training pressure cooker... ▼

Age-based horse programs can have financial benefits, but they also should come with a big warning sign: "YOU ARE PLAYING WITH FIRE."

The agendas that humans set for horses, like futurities, two-year-old racing, young jumper, young event horse, young dressage horse programs...so many of them are just that—human programs. Some horses deal well, many are pushed too soon, too hard, and some are destroyed either physically or mentally.

There are some studies that show that a degree of pressure on young bones and various other structures

Denny Emerson | *Begin and Begin Again*

helps make them stronger, while there are also plenty of youngsters that break down under stress. Humans tend to push young horses for one of several reasons:

- Money

- Impatience

- Ignorance

- Don'tgiveadamn-ism

I suspect that all of the above come into play in many cases.

There's a saying: "You can work them hard earlier. You can work them hard later. But you can't work them hard earlier and later."

Generally speaking, the horses that are given enough time to mature before they get pressured have overall longer careers than the babies who get hammered. ◆

This good trainer will perhaps think, "Does this horse understand what I am asking him to do? Is he fit enough to do it? Is he getting tired? Has he had enough calm warmup or is he tight because he is full of unspent energy?"

The good trainer will look for real answers, while the lesser trainer will go for the easy and—almost always—erroneous conclusion that the horse knows what to do, is capable of doing it, but is simply misbehaving and needs to be taught by force.

Here, though, is the problem with using force. It creates a vicious circle. The rider feels the "wrong" response from the horse, so she perhaps uses stronger aids, or gets a stronger bit, or uses leverage devices like draw reins and starts to drill and grind to force "obedience." The horse gets more scared and more uncomfortable and resists harder. The rider feels the heightened resistance and uses even more force, which creates more fear, and now the training session has only one way to go: bad, worse, terrible. And the session ends with a tired horse, an exasperated rider, and guess what? The next training session will probably be just as hard or worse, because it starts with an apprehensive horse and a rider determined to fix the problem.

Force leads to force leads to force—until the whole cycle ends, and the rider either gives up or is replaced by a more educated and sympathetic person, that horse is being driven down a rathole, and we see this every day, every place where people train horses. (For more, see "Can a Fearful Horse Learn?" p. 115.) ◆ ◆ ◆

BEGIN

to Educate Yourself

By following some of the breeding pages, I discovered how much of a split existed between horses bred for dressage and those bred for jumping.

5

_ How Educated Do You Want to Be?

Let's just take a random example. Just suppose that for some obscure reason you are part of a study group doing a discussion about South America, and each of you is assigned a country, and yours is Chile. And let's suppose that you know almost nothing about Chile, except, perhaps, you have some vague recollection that it is a long, narrow country with mountains. You don't know precisely where Chile is. You don't know what countries border it, or how large a land mass it covers, or what its population is. You don't know whether it is rural or built-up, or what people there do for work.

But we live in the age of Google. You open your laptop, punch in "Chile," and within seconds you have an overwhelming barrage of information. So you decide what you wish to know more about, and you begin to winnow through the volumes of facts, concepts, pictures, maps, and assorted bits of information, and within a couple of hours you have at least a general understanding of a topic that the day before was as

Field Notes

The Business of Stallions

... I've been able to stand several quite good racehorses, like Silver Comet here, who failed to "hit" sufficiently as racing sires but were far more than good enough as sport horse sires. This lovely stallion raced 87 times, won or placed in 47 of those starts, and won $520,492. A great athlete with the record of soundness and consistence to back it up. ▼

Ever since I was a kid I have been interested in the stallion-end of the horse-breeding business.

My first stallion, bought in 1958, when I was 16 and about to turn 17, was a little dark brown Morgan named Lippitt Raymond. Then came a 13-year gap without owning or standing a stallion until, in 1971, the year after we had moved to Strafford, Vermont, I bought Core Buff, a Thoroughbred yearling colt. For many years after that, we had an active stallion business going, with sometimes three or four at the same time, mostly Thoroughbred stakes horses that hadn't hit big enough to make it as profitable racing sires. A few names in no particular order, off the top of my head: Lord Derby, Loyal Pal, Epic Win, Silver Comet, Reputed Testamony, Forfeit, Right Of Light, Goliad, Aberjack, Formula One, Wintry Oak. We've had something like 15 stallions over the years.

At a certain point, the sheer hassle gets to the point where it makes sense to either go big or get out. All the telephone calls, the breeding contracts, the teasing mares, the semen collecting, the preparation, mixing in the extender, the shipping—the mad rush to get to the bus station or local airport, or to the FedEx office to get the shipments off in time. Anyone who has been in the business knows the drill. If you are doing all this for one stallion, you might as well do it for several, because you are just as tied to the farm and the process with one as with six, for several months, mid-spring to late summer.

We stopped standing stallions at our farms, but the business end continued to intrigue me, so I bought a yearling Thoroughbred colt, Raven Sky, and sent him to the Merle-Smith family to promote and to stand, just to keep a toehold. ◆

remote to you as some hidden valley at the bottom of the Pacific Ocean.

About 15 years ago, as the Warmblood invasion of European horses was beginning to take over the upper levels of the American English riding disciplines, I realized that I didn't know much about what a "Warmblood" was. I knew quite a bit about Morgans and Thoroughbreds. I knew a little about Irish Sport Horses. I knew the various names of the Warmblood breeds: Hanoverian, Holsteiner, Dutch Warmblood, Swedish Warmblood, Selle Français, Oldenburg, Trakehner. But I couldn't have told you much about the strengths of each Warmblood breed, who some of the successful horses were, how those breeds came to be, names of leading stallions—more than except in the most general terms. So I thought it would make sense to learn about the horses beginning to dominate the various FEI horse sports. Where did I go?

Google to the rescue. I found a bunch of websites, and if you have ever navigated Google, you know how one website will refer to you another, and each of those have links to others, in a cascading avalanche of new information.

By following some of the breeding pages, I discovered how much of a split existed between horses bred for dressage and those bred for jumping. I learned about how some stallions like Cor de la Bryère, Ladykiller, Capitol 1, and Almé had been created from lines developed after World War II, as Europe began to dig out from the rubble of destruction. I learned that breeders in the 1950s and '60s had imported Thoroughbred stallions from England and Ireland to add lightness and agility to the heavier, stronger mare lines formerly used for farm work and pulling carriages. I learned some of the names of leading sport horses such as Quidam de Revel.

I went from pretty much ignorant to knowing just enough to be dangerous, as they say. In no way did I become any sort of expert, but once I learned a few of the breeding lines I could start to use that knowledge as a base so that when I would see that such-and-such a horse had won, say, the Badminton Three-Day Event or the Grand Prix of Aachen, I could look up that horse's pedigree and start to recognize certain names.

I had gotten to the point where I could start with the stallion Ibrahim, for example, and know that he had sired Almé, who had sired the spectacular jumper Galoubet, and I had an inkling of what those horses had done. I knew that Almé was the grandsire of Quidam de Revel and I bought several horses by Beaulieu's Coolman, a son of Quidam de Revel.

As Robert Frost says in *The Road Not Taken*, "Way leads on to way." One thing leads to another, relationships begin to make sense, and that tiny thread of knowledge that was as thin as piano wire begins to take on depth and breadth.

My point here is simple: we can become about as educated about some topic as we choose to be, and all it takes is study. I hope you see how basically easy it has become to open a door that once might have seemed to be solidly shut.

‒ Staying Current: It's Pretty Simple

Here are two sentences. Each describes a hypothetical person. Does either one describe you?

"John Carter is living in the Dark Ages."

"Carol Johnson is always up on the newest fads."

It's easier to stay in the Dark Ages because it doesn't take any energy or any attempt to learn about current trends. It's a cliché to say that Grandpa is computer illiterate while his 13-year-old granddaughter is a computer whiz kid. Grandpa doesn't have to stay computer illiterate; he chooses it by his unwillingness to study new technology. But he could make another choice.

The tendency to stay in the dark versus knowing what's going on is one of the reasons so many horse people get stuck in a rut, and not just for years but for a lifetime. There are thousands of riders who learned how to ride in 1970, for example, who half a century later are using the same techniques, same kinds of tack and equipment, riding similar horses, and thinking about riding and training in the same way they have always done. The world has moved on, but they have stayed put in self-imposed ignorance. Just like the grandfather who thinks that a computer is an invention of the devil and brags that he doesn't even know how to turn one on, most of these lifelong horse owners are perfectly capable of joining the modern world. The thing is, they don't care to. Or maybe they just haven't thought about it.

Let's suppose that someone does want to break out of the rut, does want to know what's going on, is open to learning. What should he or she do?

For most situations, using Google is the easiest, fastest, and most direct line of communication with the outside world, because if Google doesn't have the answer, it can direct the seeker to another place that does. There are a number of websites with training tips and strategies that Google leads to.

Take a breed that I know about, the Morgan, and a sport that I've been involved with for 60 years, eventing. I recently Googled "Morgan Horse" and got dozens of hits—each a Morgan-related subject, whether the national association (the American Morgan Horse Association), the book *Justin Morgan Had a Horse* by Marguerite Henry, or a specific breeding farm. The point being that once I hit "Morgan Horse" on Google, I was immersed in information. I was invited to join the association. I was offered a subscription to *The Morgan Horse* magazine. I learned about Morgan farms that were open to visitors. I was given dates and locations of horse shows, which I could attend to watch Morgans in action.

Now, if I had Googled "Arabian," or "Connemara," or any other breed, I'd have been similarly guided to all sorts of resources.

Then I Googled "Sport of Eventing." Again, floods of information, including how to join the US Eventing Association, which then gives many more avenues of involvement, places to see, horse events to watch, people to meet.

Here's a Morgan mare trotting with her foal. To learn more about a specific breed, ask Google. Google will either tell you directly, or it will direct you to a site that can. Hundreds of prior generations lacked access to this cornucopia of information. Be smart. Take advantage. ◄

The easiest way to stay current in 2021 is to have a computer so you can discover various websites that provide up-to-date information on every subject you can imagine. Then all you have to do is read and look at the photos and videos that support the various articles.

Staying stuck in the Dark Ages is a choice. All you need to do is not look at your computer, not join breed or discipline associations, not go to watch horse shows or events, not get involved. Reverse that to move yourself out of the Dark Ages. It's pretty simple. ◆ ◆ ◆

BEGIN

to Accept Change

> *The best way to stop thinking about one thing is to start thinking about a different thing. A riding career can become a riding career in a different sport, or it can transform into a non-riding involvement with horses.*

6

_ Remember Cinderella?

Remember Cinderella? The girl with the glass slipper? The girl who enchanted Prince Charming at the ball, disappeared, but then was found?

There are lots of these fairy tales, and they usually end with the same seven words: "And they all lived happily ever after." And the reason they all lived happily, I suppose, is that there is just the right Prince Charming for the princess, and just the right princess for Prince Charming.

If only it were so with horses, there would be far less disappointment and struggle and frustration and anguish. The reality, with horses, is that while some are Prince Charmings and some are charming princesses, some are more like the ogre in *Jack and the Beanstalk* or the witch in *Hansel and Gretel* or the wolf in *Little Red Riding Hood*.

The horse stories don't tell us about that, though, do they? Alec Ramsey loved The Black. The Black, in his own way, loved Alec Ramsey. We imbibe these myths early—the Lone Ranger and Silver, Gene Autry and Champion, Roy Rogers and Trigger.

It's so easy to grow up with the almost automatic assumption that the right horse is a foregone conclusion. The slipper will fit. The goose will lay the golden egg. And when it doesn't transpire as we wish, hope, and assume, if the Mr. Right turns out to be, in this case, Mr. Wrong, now what? How can we even tell which horse is right or wrong when we ourselves are still inexperienced? How do we know what advice to take and what to discard?

We hear stories about famous riders who were told, "Get rid of that horse," and who persevered and were glad they did. We hear fewer stories about scared or over-mounted riders who were told, "Get rid of that horse," and who persevered, got badly scared or badly injured, and got out of horses forever. Those are not feel-good stories. Even when they are true, they don't become urban legends.

It is a hard reality to accept that more often than not, the right horse will help make one rider while the wrong horse may literally break another rider. So what are we looking for in our search for a horse that will boost us up, and what are we hoping to avoid?

- First, raw, genuine fear is to be fervently avoided.

- Second, run away from a high risk of serious injury.

- Third, do try to get a horse that is nice to ride.

It's pretty simple. Forget, at least at first, color, beauty, size, age, and breed, and look for a horse that doesn't scare you, won't hurt you, and that you like to ride. Really. How basic is that? Safe, sane, and fun. Start there. Why wouldn't you?

I know why some of you wouldn't do the commonsense thing. Here are a few reasons, virtually all of them bad ones.

- You think that somehow riding the tough horses makes you better in the long run.

Nothing, as in no other single anything, can take the place of the calm, low-key, tolerant horse in terms of providing the learning rider with a confidence-producing learning situation. These saintly horses, like the Morgan mare Roxie here, with Abby Emerson, 11, are worth their weight in your favorite flavor of Ben & Jerry's. At Morgan Heritage Days, Abby was Princess Jasmine riding Rajah. It was raining too hard to paint the stripes on Roxie, so they made do with a blanket instead. ▲ ▶

- You want a "fancy" horse to impress your friends, even if the horse is harder to ride than you are ready to deal with.

- Your trainer or best friend told you to buy a particular horse.

- This is the only available horse and "better this than nothing."

- You simply can't tell the difference yet between an easier or tougher horse.

I do believe that it is sometimes true when the former tough, gutsy little kid says, "That pony bucked me off three times a week when I was starting out, and that made me the good rider I am today." But the operative words are "sometimes true." Far more often, the riders who get bucked off, spun off, or scared off simply quit riding and do something else. They are lost to horse sports forever, and we never hear their names again.

Beginners make mistakes because that is what beginners do. And here's the thing that separates a beginner in riding from, say, a beginner in golf, or a beginner at playing the piano. The golf club doesn't care if you miss the ball. The piano doesn't care if you hit the wrong note. They are inanimate objects and don't respond in a negative way, not the way a horse or a dog or another human might respond if dealt with badly.

It stands to reason, then, that since a beginner rider will make mistakes, the ideal horse to begin riding on will be a tolerant horse who lets the rider get away with those mistakes. We want a non-reactive, "low-octane" horse who doesn't get too bothered when the rider does something wrong, and it is guaranteed that the novice rider will do something wrong. So this is where you should start, by finding a horse with a nice, even, nonconfrontational temperament.

What does "temperament" mean in horse terms? I have used a one-to-10 scale for years, a "one" being an entirely phlegmatic, non-reactive, totally low-key animal, and a "10" being a virtually unrideable hot mess. In broad brush strokes, the lower the number, the calmer and steadier the horse. By my calculations, horses that have temperaments in the one-to-four range are likely to tolerate our mistakes. They are more apt to stand still while we mount and dismount. They don't jig and dance and prance. They are not inclined to take off suddenly, or to spook and spin out from under us at a kid on a bike or a piece of flapping plastic stuck to a bush. At the trot and canter, these lower-key horses are not apt to grab the bit and speed up. The ones and twos, on the contrary, are apt to slow down, and even to stop, if we don't keep urging them to go.

The point here is that a rider is a lot less likely to get scared or hurt on a one, two, three, or four than on a flighty, nervous, reactive seven, eight, or nine. So much of the angst and tension and nervousness that we see every day in the relationships between humans and horses could be alleviated by having the rider who needs a two or three actually ride a two or a three instead of white-knuckling it on an unsuitable six or seven, or God forbid, a flaming eight or nine. Never mind the 10. If you get on a 10, you get a free ride to the emergency room.

Sometimes the green rider is so inexperienced that she can't tell the difference between a steady horse and a hot one, and this is where it makes sense to get some advice from someone with more of a riding background. But this implies that humans will take good advice. There's a sort of joke that goes like this: "The only people who will take your advice are the ones who agreed with you before you gave it."

So, be smart or be otherwise. It's a choice. If you get to ride the right horse for your current level, you will have more fun and you will improve faster than you will on a horse that you can't ride very well.

Why Is Change So Hard?

Anyone who has made a New Year's resolution only to see it shattered days later knows that change is easy to talk about but hard to do.

If we look to science for answers, we are told about neurons and neurotransmitters and synaptic connections and ways in which the brain is wired, including neuroplasticity, the ability of the brain to change. Science tells us that change is not a lightning bolt

Field Notes
The Benefits of Patience

_ This pretty young Thoroughbred mare, Frosty Lover, is demonstrating that in "real life," the transformation from racehorse to riding sport horse can be more of a challenge than "they" tell you about. Strength and fitness to carry herself in balance has to be gradually built in. It doesn't come floating down from the sky like manna from heaven. When Frosty feels different pressure than she has been used to on the track, up goes the head. It's a huge mistake to equate this normal questioning resistance with "being bad." Frosty just doesn't understand, and I have to gently negotiate with her, allowing her all the time that she needs. ▼

In daily training, and especially in the case of young ex-racehorses like this young mare, there is not going to be instant harmony and calm acceptance of working from behind, over the back, into a quiet and steady connection with the bit.

Some people who are not trainers, and don't know the long, slow process of retraining a horse with a worried mouth and head and neck connection, will see pictures like these and fling themselves to the ground, frothing at the mouth and writhing in self-righteous indignation at "what the poor horse is forced to endure." It's one of the reasons that so much poor horsemanship exists. Who wants to try to educate people that clueless and catch all the flack?

Denny Emerson | *Begin and Begin Again*

This seemingly simple process may well take months, because several things need to change.

The horse has to learn to trust that I am not going to hurt her, that's a big one right there. Next, it will take lots of time for her to get stronger, and until she does that, she will lack balance: her head will go up—then a moment of sort of okay—then behind the vertical—above, behind, okay, fuss, fuss, fuss.

The main job that I have, as trainer, is to put my head in "emotional neutral," because she has no agenda to "be bad," and to get after her would only trigger more anxiety.

With the quick and hard head flippers, I often use a loose running martingale, because who wants a bloody nose? But only for that, never to lever the head down.

How long will this take? As long as it takes. ◈

but a process through stages, from precontemplation, to contemplation, to preparation, to action stage, to maintenance stage. This is from an article in *Psychology Today* by Katherine Schreiber.

Any teacher can tell stories about smart students who failed and about those with average intelligence who excelled. It's the same in riding as in teaching a scholastic subject.

You, I, we, the students, can be taught all sorts of skill sets that we need in order to improve. We can be told that we need to become fitter and stronger athletes. We can be exhorted to be more persistent, to be more patient, to work harder, to study more diligently, to gain more empathy for the horses that we ride and handle. Every bit of this teaching that is ladled out to us is based on the supposition that we are willing or able to change.

Just about every smoker that I personally know absolutely grasps the fact that smoking is a bad habit, that it is a health risk, that it is expensive, that it smells bad. They all want to quit, and yet many of them keep smoking. Alcoholics keep drinking. Those who don't like to exercise keep sitting. The world is filled with examples of people who desperately need to change in order not to be sick and die, and yet can't manage to change even to save their own lives.

So, if change is that hard, why should we even bother to try? One reason to try is that we all know people who *have* quit smoking, *have* stopped drinking, *have* gotten off drugs, *have* lost weight and kept it off, *have* become more active. Change is definitely hard, but it is not impossible. So that's one good reason.

Another reason to try is for the good of the horses we ride. We say that we love horses, so we should prove it. Learn patience. Study better training methods. Become a softer, more balanced rider. If not for our own sakes, for theirs.

To stay put means to keep doing the same thing in the same way at the same level. Some of us derive great pleasure from the security of finding a slot and staying there, some feel stuck in a rut with boredom, while others might feel apprehension at being in over their heads.

If you are loving it, why change? Keep on keeping on until or unless something makes you either want to change or have to change. You do this for you, after all.

In horse sports, the phrase "to move up" means to take on a higher or harder or more technical degree of challenge. Many horse sports have clearly defined levels, and each level has clearly defined and mostly objective standards.

A dressage rider who moves from First-Level tests to Second-Level tests is moving up. An event rider who is competing at the Novice Level may feel ready to move up to the Training Level. An endurance rider who has been doing what are called "limited distance" rides may feel ready to move up to 50-mile competition. In foxhunting, which is not a competition, someone who has been riding as a hill-topper may feel that the time has come to move up to second field.

In order to make these moves work out well, the rider and the horse should be comfortable with the heightened requirements. I wouldn't want to move from Novice eventing, where the maximum fence heights are 2 feet 11 inches, up to Training, which has heights of up to 3 feet, 3 inches, if my horse couldn't handle that 4-inch difference without hitting the rails or sometimes refusing to jump.

Many instructors will actually hold riders back from moving up a level until the horse-and-rider team seems more than ready and is practicing things at home that are harder to do than what's being asked at the next level. In risk sports like eventing or foxhunting, where horses have to jump solid fences, where the top rails can't be knocked out of the cups, it is more important to be almost more than ready than it is in sports like dressage, where lack of success may humiliate you but won't actually hurt you.

If you feel like moving up in some horse sport and you think you're ready, and you feel confident, try it and see how it goes. You can always move back down if you don't like it up there. But what if you don't like where you are right now? Just as you can stay put or move up, so you can move down a level or two. Try not to be shamed by others, or by your own expectations, into staying at a level that makes you uncomfortable or unsuccessful. Remember who you do this for, right? You do this for yourself. Not for your mother. Not for your teacher. Not for your friend Sally. You are doing this because you want to do this for you. It can be amazingly liberating to finally realize that fact if you have been letting the expectations you've put upon yourself trap you in a place you don't like.

Moving sideways, in the context I'm talking about, means moving from one type of riding or horse-related activity to a different one.

There are thousands of examples of how this can happen. You've been playing polo and you want to try foxhunting. You've been foxhunting and you want to try eventing. You've been eventing and you want to try dressage. You've been doing English dressage and you want to try Western dressage. You've been doing Western dressage and you want to try reining. You've been doing reining and you want to try cutting.

You've been doing cutting and you decide to try polo.

See? You can go full circle if that's what makes you happy.

Don't be surprised if a sideways move also necessitates a downward move. The new way makes you a novice, and though your overall experience may make you a quick study, give yourself some leeway to get used to the new way.

⸺ Coming to Grips with Diminished Ability

Nothing lasts forever. Athletic careers are fragile and finite, and at some point, skills and strength fade. This can happen in a matter of seconds, in the case of a bad accident, or it can take decades, but it will happen.

When it does, how are you going to deal with the new reality?

Bart Giamatti was the seventh Commissioner of Major League Baseball. Within five months of becoming commissioner, he died of a heart attack at 51. He had been trying to figure out ways to prevent former major league players from slipping into depression, eating disorders, and alcoholism after retiring from baseball. Giamatti pointed out that most of these players had been the center of attention from their first days in Little League, when they so completely overpowered and outshone the other kids. As they got older, this became more pronounced. Headlines, photos in newspapers and magazines, contracts, signing bonuses, baseball cards, television, the roar of the crowd.

Suddenly it all stops. Now what? Except for the few superstars, in five years, 10 at the outside, most of those men were "out of sight, out of mind."

These are perhaps extreme examples, but the basic situation can apply to the rider who used to bravely gallop down the beach, wind in her hair, and now has trouble getting on her horse at a mounting block.

Do you retire or do you adapt? I suggest that you adapt. This book is about adapting and changing, and adapting should not be thought of as surrendering.

When you are finished with one chapter, open a new chapter, and become immersed in that.

The best way to stop thinking about one thing is to start thinking about a different thing. A riding career can become a riding career in a different sport, or it can transform into a non-riding involvement with horses. Just because you are not the Valkyrie you were at 18 doesn't mean that your days with horses should be tossed out the window. This may take a new kind of courage—but it always took courage.

Be brave.

_ Stages of Recovery from Injury

Anyone who has been injured badly enough to have spent time in a hospital will know that there can be any number of stages to get through on the road to physical and emotional recovery. There are so many variables, and there's no one-size-fits-all formula for becoming whole again. A healthy young person will generally recover faster than someone who is older and less fit. A broken wrist gets better faster than a broken hip. A sort of daredevil, high-risk person will bounce back mentally and emotionally far sooner than someone who was already timid before the accident. And so on.

The key variable is the severity of the injury and the prognosis for recovery. There are two kinds of injuries that can be especially

_ You can leap into water "at Mach 2, with your hair on fire" in one part of your riding career, and you can stroll through water in another phase of your riding life. You know the saying, "Whatever floats your boat." Maybe, "Whatever floats your horse" is the better description. ▲ ▶

devastating: head injuries causing brain damage, and spinal cord injuries that cause paralysis. It's hard to even talk about these because sometimes there just isn't any good outcome. Not for someone whose head injury changes her life forever. So I won't go there, except to say this: Wear a helmet.

But let's assume that the injury will not cause too much long-term damage, that even though there might be months of rehab coming up, there is light at the end of the tunnel. Now what?

Well, for me, when I had a broken neck from a fall, and before that, when on two occasions I broke first my right hip, and later, my left hip, the first thing is giving yourself permission to rest long enough, whether for a few days or some months, for the initial trauma to subside. Let yourself sleep. Let yourself grieve and regret. Later you can start to claw yourself out of your pain and misery, but it's not always a quick fix, so don't try to force it.

Don't give in to a desperate need to get instantly back to normal. Actually listen to your doctor and nurses and your rehab people. You might not like the timetable they lay out, but try not to fight them tooth and nail. They are not "the enemy." They are not antagonists to whom you have to "prove something."

There's a fine line between resting enough to let the trauma subside and letting lethargy engulf you. At some point you are going to have restart your engines, and part of what makes this so hard is that it hurts and you are weak. "Weak" and "in pain" are a bad combination, but if that's your reality, at some point, you will need to start fighting, unless you don't care if your recovery takes forever.

This is where your rehab team can guide you. They are trained professionals, and though they will push you, they know better than you how much is enough and how much is too much.

One part of the equation: Are you on crutches or a walker because of a lower-body injury, or was it your upper body, and can you still walk? Because in either case, there are uninjured parts of you that you can still strengthen. Walking on crutches is good exercise and so is walking without crutches. Within reason, the more you can start to struggle back to general fitness, the better, and this means if you are able to do things that make you pant, and that get your heart rate up, you are doing your body some good. But don't be foolish and do too much. When in doubt, ask those who know more.

I think it's better to exercise more often, in briefer chunks, with rest periods, than to try to go all out. Push yourself, but don't hurt yourself. Have patience with the process. Fitness doesn't come swiftly even if you haven't been hurt, so try to think of your recovery as a journey rather than a destination. It's hard, and there will be times of despair. That's just how it is, I found. But there will be a day that you notice you can do what before you could not do, and these times will become more frequent. You are healing, and your body is getting stronger, and just knowing that will give you the boost you need to keep going.

So, that's some of the physical recovery. Now, what about the emotional part? Of course, if you are lucky, you won't have residual fear. You won't relive your accident over and over, or wake up in a sweat, full of terror the way we see it happening in the movies to soldiers who have PTSD from battle. But you also might have lingering fear or, if not outright fear, you may have strong doubts about whether you will ever be confident enough to ride again.

So right here, a disclaimer: I am not in any way trained to give advice about Post-Traumatic Stress Disorder. If you are haunted, get professional help.

For me, the one thing that *was* in my control was to work hard physically to get fitter and stronger so that when I did decide to get back on a horse, I'd have the confidence of knowing that I was tough enough to be ready to ride, even though I knew I would be rusty. I worked in the woods, clearing riding trails, cutting and hauling saplings into brush piles, sawing small logs. Sometimes I'd have to stop and pant, but then I would dig in again.

After I broke my neck in 2011, and three weeks later spent my seventieth birthday in a halo, I was only able to hike for the first three months after the accident. Then, when I was out of the halo and was given the green light by the doctor to do more, I started with the trail clearing.

...I trusted Atti not to pull some stunt or antic or have a quick reaction to a chirping sparrow. Could she have proved me wrong? Sure. There's no such thing as a fool-proof horse, not even the mechanical one at Walmart, but you gotta start again somewhere! ▶

And when I finally felt ready to ride again—are you listening?—I chose the calmest, quietest, most reliable horse on the farm—Atti, a big Warmblood mare—because I trusted her to just walk around and not try anything stupid or dramatic. The last thing I needed was to have a fall from a spook. I wasn't "scared" but I was damn cautious. The good news was that after a few days of just walking for 15-20-30 minutes, I felt comfortable enough to go on some longer walking trail rides. From there, I built up to some slow trotting. I did not have any timetable or agenda, I didn't need to please anyone but myself, and I took as long as it took.

Here's what I think you need to understand: This is *your* recovery. It isn't your doctor's. It isn't your family's. It isn't anyone else's but yours. You can come back a little, a lot, or all the way, but do what you want on the timetable that you set.

Starting over after a bad accident or after a severe illness is the hardest start-over you will ever do. If you can do this, anything else is just a piece of cake with chocolate frosting and vanilla ice cream. ◆ ◆ ◆

BEGIN

to Train with Intention

Let go of the thoughts in your busy head so you can feel the release in your riding body, to be one with the horses you ride.

7

_ The Paradigm Shift

A paradigm shift happens when there is some sort of incident or discovery or revelation so intense and powerful that it can absolutely change the fundamental truth that one held as a belief into an opposite or contrasting one.

Here is an example I've read about: A ship is traveling at night. The signalman sees another ship in the distance, directly in front of his ship. He flashes a signal to the other ship, "Steer to starboard 40 degrees."

The second ship flashes back, "No, *you* steer 40 degrees starboard."

The first ship flashes again, "No, you change course. This ship carries the Admiral of the Fleet."

The second ship flashes back, "Negative. YOU steer 40 degrees to starboard. This is a lighthouse."

Field Notes

Distance
and Jumping

_ Riders like Daryl Kinney here (foreground) walk courses before they jump them for several reasons. The first is simply to remember where they have to go, the sequence of the fences in the course. The more sophisticated riders also are able to assess the number of feet (meters in some countries) between jumps, which allows them to adjust their horse's canter stride for greater accuracy. ▼

Let's talk about jumping from a distance that gives the horse a fighting chance of having a successful jump.

Here we come at a canter or gallop. Looming closer is a vertical post-and-rail fence that is, say, 3 feet, 9 inches high. Years of actual observation tells us that right around 6 feet in front of the jump is not too close, not too far away.

If the horse gets to a point that is, let's say, 5 feet away, or 7 feet away, he can still probably struggle over, depending on his speed, balance, and impulsion. But if he gets to a takeoff point that is 4 feet away, or closer, he will do one of three things:

1. He will stop.

2. He will jump but hit the fence.

3. He will do a "helicopter jump"—straight up, straight down—not hitting the fence.

Denny Emerson | *Begin and Begin Again*

So, if the fence is in cups, a show-jumping post and rail, and he hits it, no big deal, because he knocks the rail out of the cups with no bad repercussions, except in the truly rare times he might get tangled with the loose rail. If it's a solid fence and he hits it below his knees, he may stumble, he may trip and fall, but he usually gets away with it.

It gets dicey when he hits it above his knees. If the fence rail doesn't break, the horse's forward motion is stopped dead, and his momentum can cause what we call a "rotational fall" where the horse essentially somersaults over the fence and crashes to the ground, potentially lethal for both rider and horse.

But what happens when the horse gets to a takeoff point that is farther away than about 7 feet? What usually happens is that the horse will try to jam in another stride, what is called, in jumping terminology, a "chip stride." Now we are right back where we were before, too close to the fence, so all those things we just talked about apply. So how do we avoid too many wrong distances?

Well, one way is to leave it up to the horse, hoping that the horse will save himself. Some horses will, some horses won't, and some horses do it some of the time but not always.

Okay, so what about having the rider "help" the horse? Some riders are sort of born with such depth perception that they can just tell whether to stay, shorten, or lengthen. Some riders can sort of "feel" the distance. Some riders jump about a million small fences until they can recognize the distance. There is no right or wrong way to do it. It depends upon what works for you. And the way to find that out is by getting a good teacher, and riffling through the pack of cards, so to speak, to find the hand that works best for your situation.

What I do know is this: if you are on a galloping horse, and you are coming along at a solid cross-country fence "blind as a bat," you are in over your head, and you are asking for it. ◆

When I first started jumping, way back in 1961, there was a kind of standard truth that got repeated. It had to do with whether a rider was able to "see a distance" in front of a jump, and thus able to adjust his horse's stride in order to "get to a good takeoff spot." The truth, or conventional wisdom, was phrased, "You are either born with a good eye or you're not."

The point was that if you couldn't tell how far you were away from getting to an ideal takeoff spot, generally around 6 feet in front of a jump—the distance from which it is most easy for the horse to navigate the jump—you were doomed for life to having to deal with takeoff spots that were less than ideal. You had to hope that your horse would adjust himself or that you could survive being some of the time too close to the jump or too far away from it. If your horse did arrive at the ideal distance, it would be by blind luck, or because the horse saw the distance and had adjusted his own stride.

Nobody ever told me otherwise. Nobody ever said, "Denny,

while it is true that some riders are born with the ability to see a distance, just because you are not one of those riders does not mean that there are not alternative methods to develop the ability to get your horse to a good takeoff spot *most of the time*."

And so for more than a decade, I struggled along with the idea fixed in my mind that while some lucky few could get their horses to good takeoff spots, I would never be one of them.

I did pretty well in spite of not having a good eye for a distance. I was young and strong and fit, agile and athletic, and I was usually able to deal with not-so-great distances by staying out of my horse's way and letting him deal.

The place where it hurt my scores the most was in the show-jumping phase in eventing. Points are deducted for rails that get knocked down, and a horse is more

likely to hit a rail from arriving too far away from a jump, or too close to a jump, than from being just right.

I even was on the United State Equestrian Team's gold-medal eventing squad in the 1974 World Championships without having an eye for a distance. My paradigm shift happened sometime in the mid-1970s, in the most unlikely way.

A monthly magazine called *Practical Horseman* would sometimes have experts write long "how-to" articles about various techniques or training methods. One such article was about show jumping, and it was written by my long-time friend Bernie Traurig. Bernie had won the big equestrian championships, the Medal and the Maclay, as a teenager, and he had become one of America's top Grand-Prix jumping riders.

This, in general terms, was the paragraph in Bernie's article that was to lead to my epiphany about seeing

⌐ Bernie Traurig is a sort of Thomas Jefferson of English riding. He was an equitation champion, was on the USET eventing squad, then on the USET show jumping squad, raced over brush and timber, and rode Grand Prix level dressage. Now he educates, through clinics and through his vast teaching website. Here's Bernie evaluating a horse-and-rider team in 2021. ▲

a distance. It went something like this: "There will almost always be places during a show-jumping round where you will be approaching a jump that is parallel to your horse. If you can learn to see three strides off your turn to the fence, you will never have to worry about those kinds of turns again."

For some reason, this appealed to me. Perhaps it was because of the exactitude of "three strides"—a specific number, a definite goal.

For whatever reason, I thought to myself, "I'm going to play around with this. I probably can't do it because I wasn't born with a good eye, but it might be fun to try." Or something like that.

So, I would canter along on a path parallel to a jump, and when I thought it looked like it might be three strides away, I would swing my horse toward the fence and say "one, two, three." Or maybe "three, two, one" and see what happened.

And what happened amazed me. As I practiced and practiced, I began to recognize what three strides in front of a jump looked like. The more I practiced, the more I recognized it. I could not "just see it," but I could learn to recognize a distance on the ground that represented three strides. I was learning to see my distance in a different way.

So I thought, well, if I can see three strides off a turn, why can't I see three strides coming straight at the fence? I started to look for three strides coming perpendicular to the jump, and lo and behold, I could. And the more I practiced, the easier it got. And over time, three strides became four strides, even five.

All those years of doing it wrong, of drinking the Kool-Aid, changed in 30 seconds by reading one paragraph in a magazine article.

Please listen carefully to what I am going to say: People will tell you in a hundred ways why you can't do something. They will tell you that you are too young, too old, too short, too fat, too thin, too timid, too this, too that, and they will try to make you believe it, and if you do believe it, you will never know whether what they told you was impossible is actually impossible, or just somebody else trying to put limits on you.

If you buy into some other person's negative assessment, pretty soon it becomes *your* negative assessment, and this can be as totally mistaken as my assumption that "because I was not born with a good eye, I could never have a good eye." When someone tells you what you can't do, they may be right, but they may just as easily be wrong. I think that lots of our acquaintances, even our friends, even our well-meaning families, have certain ideas about what is and isn't possible, and they unconsciously try to impose their own limitations on others.

— Components of Training

So, base fitness in place, we can be more confident about the teaching components of training. One of the best ways to think about being a horse trainer is to think of yourself as a first-grade teacher of six-year-old children. These kids can't read or spell or add or subtract. They don't even know letters, never mind words, and they don't know numbers. A little kid can't add one and one to make two until he learns what one means. He can't spell "cat" until he learns the alphabet. A horse trainer is like the first-grade teacher, because the trainer is teaching a language. First, he teaches the horse what "A" means. Then "B." And so on. But, because horses are pretty much nonverbal, the horse trainer doesn't "talk" to the horse with vocal cords, but with a system of pressure and release by hands, legs, arms, seat, all of which substitute for letters, words, and sentences.

We call this system of mostly nonverbal communication "aids." Aids are, like words to humans, a means of communication. We have to teach the horse the "language" of aids. Some riders never develop an extensive language, so they don't have much to teach the horse. For these lowest-level riders, a kick or a whack with a stick means "go." A pull or a yank on the reins means "stop." Or "slow down." A pull on the left rein means "turn left." A pull on the right rein means "turn right." And that about does it for thousands of riders who either have little interest in taking horse training beyond the bare basics or simply don't know any better. More sophisticated riders install a more sophisticated language.

_ "Tense," by Jockey Club name, but not by nature. Tense raced 34 times, earned about $50,000 and retired sound. Retraining him is still an ongoing process, but much of the racing-induced tightness and inelasticity is being replaced by a more supple acceptance of the new type of work. ▶

_ Teach Those Basics Quietly

When a rider gets tight, rigid, and demanding while teaching these responses, most horses react by getting tense and nervous. The rigid rider will create a rigid, resistant horse. This often results in blaming the horse. "This horse isn't doing what I want. This horse is being bad." And the moment the blame game comes into play, it only goes downhill from there.

The most athletic and successful riders are what we might call "slithery." Now I am fully aware that few books about horse training, especially books about dressage, talk about the need for a slithery rider. But they should, because a slithery, slinky, elastic rider is the opposite of a tight, rigid, tense rider, and the same horse who tenses up at rigidity will breathe a great sigh of relief when he feels negotiated and elastic coaxing instead of tight, coercive demanding. Picture the way a jungle cat slinks through tall grass, or the way a snake writhes, curls, folds and unfolds. There is little about these images that appears constrained or fraught with tension.

When a rider gets on a horse thinking, "This horse must do what I want, when I want, and how I want," there is a guaranteed

Field Notes

Our Inner Dialogue Matters

The words that we think in our heads will have quite an impact on our training sessions.

Here is an example: I am trying to get my horse to come from a canter to a trot without curling his head or inverting his head. (There are hundreds of similar examples, don't get fixated on this one.) Anyway, let's say that he either curls or inverts.

So, in my head I say, "This horse won't..." Or I can just as readily say, "This horse isn't..."

When I say to myself, "This horse won't...," I am assigning motive and blame. It's almost the same as saying, "He could if he wanted to, but he's being a jerk about this." And this gives me a sort of "permission to punish." And we know what a rabbit hole that turns into.

If I say to myself, "This horse isn't...," I am simply stating a fact. It allows me space to ask, "Why isn't he? Is he too green for this much of a transition? Are my aids unclear? Are my arms too tight? Is this the best bit to be using?" and so on.

Inner dialogue: Positive or negative? And you bet it matters. ◆

— Lila Gendal and Beaulieu's Cool Skybreaker in a contemplative moment. How we think determines how we will act. How we act will determine how the horse responds. It behooves us to get our thinking straight before we translate thought to action. ▼

fight waiting to happen. The horse is a prey animal, a creature of flight. The overly demanding rider becomes like the mountain lion that has leapt off the rock, and while the horse may not react with total panic, as he would if attacked by a lion, the same principle applies.

What if that rider took a totally different approach, and thought, "Well this horse doesn't know about legs, or hands, or seat, or weight distribution, so I need to be super careful that I don't create fear and tension by asking very much?"

What if the rider realizes that, just as the first-grade human child needs to learn the alphabet before she can make little words, so the horse needs to be taught what various pressures and releases by the rider are asking the horse to do? Instead of A-B-C-D, the rider might use a bit of leg pressure to mean "move forward," a bit of rein pressure to mean "stop." Or a light pull and softening on the left rein to mean "turn left," and the same on the right rein to mean "turn right." All of this will be done calmly, quietly, gently, so as not to trigger anxiety, because there is no horse that is elastic and slinky and bendable physically if he is not all those things emotionally. An anxious, nervous horse will not be and cannot be as flexible and elastic and athletic as a calm horse, and the only way—the *only* way—to create calmness is to avoid doing things that make the horse anxious.

You can't get rid of anxiety by being too demanding. You can't get rid of anxiety by working the horse halfway to exhaustion. You can't get rid of anxiety by using bitting rigs or draw reins or stronger bits. The only way that a rider can get rid of anxiety and tension in a horse is by using riding and training strategies that don't trigger much tension.

Yes, a tough, demanding, forceful rider can make a horse obey, to some degree, but the forced horse will never perform as well, or anywhere near as reliably, as the horse that has been quietly taught correct responses. So, it becomes very simple. The good trainers teach the horse to do it. The bad trainers make the horse do it.

Force (Almost) Never Comes from a Good Place

Under what conditions and circumstances is force justified? Here are a couple of examples, one on the ground, the other on the horse's back.

I am leading a horse in from the paddock to the barn on a chilly, windy day. The horse is leaping and kicking out behind, and if he gets too far away from me on one of those leaps, gets his rear end toward me, and gives a double-barrel kick, he can literally kill me. Am I going to let him do that, or am I going to put a chain over his nose, or a knotted rope halter, or something that when I take a sharp tug on it, he respects it, and stops with the airs above the ground? You can be Mr. Nice Guy and let him pull that sort of stuff, but I won't take the chance.

The Alexander the Great and the Gordian Knot School of Horse Starting

There was an intricate, tangled knot, called the Gordian Knot, and legend had it that whoever could untie the knot would become ruler of Asia.

Alexander studied the knot, saw what a long, tedious process it represented, drew his sword, and slashed through the knot. Done, finished, mission accomplished.

Many horses are like that Gordian Knot: knots of tangled emotion, either because they are unhandled, or because they've been roughly handled, and years ago, it was pretty typical "wisdom" that you would rope the horse, slap a saddle on him while he was tightly confined, have someone grab an ear while some tough kid climbed on, and let the horse and rider fight it out until the horse was subdued—a sort of Alexander the Great solution, no finesse, brutal and swift.

The riders who could do this were considered the best of the best, and it was actually scorned in some riding cultures if someone took the time to gentle a horse. A horse who didn't buck was dismissed as a "lady's" horse, whereas the macho thing was to be able to dominate the horse. Pretty Dark Ages thinking, but even in 2021, vestiges of those old attitudes still hang on in some places.

Untangling the fears and resistances of troubled horses requires huge patience and the willingness to try to keep below the horse's anxiety threshold, and it's not a quick-fix sort of deal. ◆

— When Alexander slashed the Gordian knot, he got the job done in the least subtle way possible. We read about horse breakers who tie wild horses to snubbing posts, strap saddles to their trembling flanks, climb aboard, and buck them out—the Gordian knot school of breaking, quick and brutal. I guess some riders still do this. The good ones don't. ▼

Denny Emerson | *Begin and Begin Again*

So that's one example of using a degree of force to preserve my safety.

Here's another: I am galloping a strong, exuberant Thoroughbred on a hard cross-country course. His blood is up. The sheer speed feeds his aggression, and he starts to haul me out of the tack. His adrenaline is blotting out his self-preservation instinct as he comes fast and flat toward a solid fence. If I need to ride this horse in a Pelham, or some other sort of bit, with more leverage than a simple snaffle, and if I have to sit up, brace my heels, and haul on him, if that's what it takes to keep him from eating some fence for lunch, I am darn well going to do it.

So, there are two examples where, for the sake of my safety, the use of force is justified, in my opinion. But except for those kinds of situations, I have come to realize that use of force of almost any kind is a one-way downhill slide.

Think about it: what are the primary "ingredients" of a tractable, well-trained horse?

Well, first of all, the horse is not hot, nervous, anxious, or scared, because a horse that has any of those negative qualities doesn't process the aids of the rider well.

The well-trained horse isn't some beaten-down creature that has been cowed into abject submission. Sure, if a hard-nosed human uses enough brutal force for long enough, that can produce a horse that has what is called "learned helplessness," total submission, all spirit extinguished. But

is that stunned robot what we think of as a well-trained horse? Because if that is your idea of training, our ideas are so far apart that we can't even agree to disagree.

Let's assume, though, that we agree that mashing all the life and spark out of a horse is not part of correct training, and then let's look at the way force prevents what we are trying to achieve.

I think we should approach this by asking a question: "How well does a fearful horse learn?"

Can a Fearful Horse Learn?

One way to grasp this is to think of yourself sitting in an airplane, trying to learn about some topic by reading about it. The plane is cruising smoothly, the flight attendant is coming along the aisles passing out coffee or ginger ale, all is calm. You can concentrate on your reading and grasp its content.

Now, suddenly, the captain's voice comes on the intercom: "Passengers, please return to your seats and fasten your seatbelt. We are about to enter some possibly strong turbulence."

The plane starts to lurch and buck in a violent thunderstorm. How much effective studying are you getting done now?

Okay, so how much information can a scared horse process? Is he learning or is he reacting? And here's where it gets worse. The horse is nervous because of *something*. It can be for any of dozens of reasons, doesn't really matter what, and because he's nervous, anxious, downright scared, what does he do?

We know what he does. He reacts in ways that we can easily call "disobedience." He is "being bad." Or he is "being naughty." Or he is "being a brat." So, to fix the resistance that stemmed from some sort of anxiety, the rider uses more pressure, more force. So the horse gets more afraid, more hesitant. So the rider uses even more force, maybe hauls out a stronger bit or some other leverage device such as draw-reins.

Is use of force really going to get rid of the horse's nervousness? Are you joking? It's obviously going to make it worse and worse. It has no place to go but downhill. And that is the secret about using force on a horse, any time, any place, for almost any reason. The more force you use, the more scared he gets. The more scared he gets, the more he resists. The more he resists, the more force you use....

See where this is going? Your only hope is to feel that original nervous tension and to instantly think, "Why? Why is my horse responding this way? Is he hurting in some way? If so, where and why? Or is my riding confusing him? Am I asking something he doesn't understand? Am I driving him too hard? Is he getting tired, frustrated, anxious?"

Your only hope is to find the real reason and start by trying to fix it. No force. Don't go there. Don't start that snowball rolling.

_ Long-Lining—Ground-Driving

During June, July, and August of 1961, the summer between my sophomore and junior years at Dartmouth College, I worked as a very lowly assistant trainer for Art Titus at the Green Mountain Stock Farm in Randolph, Vermont, home of the Lippitt Morgans.

Robert Lippitt Knight, the owner and breeder of Morgans with his "Lippitt" prefix, had about 50 horses on the farm, and five of them were yearling stallions. Art gave me the job of teaching them to "ground drive." Art spent a couple of hours showing me how to do it, and then left it up to me to drive each of the five horses for 15 to 20 minutes, three days a week.

... Art Titus was a quiet and "not much drama" trainer, as at home behind a horse as a reinsman as he was when he rode. I was 19, about to turn 20, the summer that I worked for him, and I am pretty sure that he was happy to let me climb on the potentially explosive babies! He took the time to explain—a good mentor to be around. ▲

... This group shot of some of us at the Green Mountain Stock Farm was taken in the summer of 1961. Left to right: farm manager Jack Esser, Kneeland Olmstead (I think), Mr. Robert Lippitt Knight, Susan Esser, me, and head trainer Art Titus. We worked together, but best of all, we were friends who liked each other. ▼

Here's how it worked: All of the babies were halter trained as weanlings to lead, to stand, and to follow a human. The next step was to get them to accept a little surcingle around their bellies, placed around where you would put a saddle. First, I would let the colt sniff the surcingle while I held it. Then I would quietly rub the surcingle all over his body, to get him used to having it touch his back, his sides. I had John, another young guy who worked there, hold the colt while I fished the girth from under his stomach so the colt could feel the pressure around his body. Some of them just stood there, no big deal; one got antsy, but soon settled; but one little chestnut sort of freaked out when he felt me start to tighten the belly cinch, and with him, it took much more time before he settled.

There were rings about mid-body on each side of the surcingle, and we had two long leather driving reins with snaps on one end. We threaded the reins through the rings and hitched the snaps to the halter. Art didn't believe in using a bit until the horses drove calmly off just halter pressure.

Then John would lead the colt around a big oval-shaped area with high wooden

Some call it "long-lining," while others call this "ground-driving." The nice part about this exercise is that you can introduce the horse to all sorts of potentially spooky objects, and he can't buck you off or spin you off, because you aren't on. This is me with Roxie, reins through her tied-down stirrups. A nice technique to learn. ▲ ◄

fencing, and I would walk behind, a rein in each hand, and I also carried a driving whip. I tried to stay just back far enough out of kicking range, but close enough to encourage the colt forward with a cluck and maybe a light touch of the whip on his rump. In addition to rein pressure, I used my voice, "whoa," "walk," to help him understand.

With John leading and me steering, we started in that confined space, steering right and left, and stopping, all of this at a walk. Once the baby got used to it, John took off the lead rope, but kept walking beside the colt, gradually getting farther away until he was out of the picture and I was steering and stopping the colt by rein and cluck aids.

I never made it out of the arena with the little chestnut colt, but the other four got quiet enough so that before long I could drive them all around the farm, letting them see the world.

Mr. Knight died the following summer, and all the Lippitt Morgans went through a sale in September 1962, so I never knew where my colts ended up. But in the 60 years since I learned that ground-driving technique, I have used it time and again to start younger horses, usually, though, at the age of two rather than at one year.

If you don't own a surcingle or driving reins, you can substitute any saddle by tying the stirrups to the girth with a couple of pieces of baling twine or string, and by using a couple of longe lines that you put through the stirrups instead of through the sewn-on rings of the surcingle. Proceed exactly the same way.

The horses can't buck you off, because you aren't on. They get used to starting, steering, and stopping, and they can be driven all over the place, getting used to plastic-covered hay bales, farm equipment, chickens, piles of lumber, puddles—so many scary realities of life in the fast lane.

You can learn this quite easily, as I did, but get a good helper, as I had, and see if you don't find that it makes starting youngsters both easier and much, much, safer.

Not an Iron Fist

Horse trainers and horse riders need to clearly and objectively think through one of the fundamental internal contradictions that exist in the world of humans and horses.

On the one hand, to have maximum physical efficiency, the rider needs to be a strong, fit, elastic, and gritty athlete. But as a species, horses are creatures of flight, prey animals rather than predators. If we let our tough physicality override our compassion and empathy, we will be just another predator, as far as the horse sees us.

I've talked about how horses do not learn through fear. Put another way, horses do learn through fear, but they do not learn to become cooperative and willing athletic partners through fear and coercion-based training strategies. And we don't really

— Having horses living outdoors, especially 24/7 turnout, is simply not an option for barns on limited acreage. Other horse owners feel it to be too risky. My take, though, is damned if you do, damned if you don't. They get hurt turned out, they get hurt or sick in the barn. Nature designed horses to live outdoors, so when possible, that's my personal go-to preference. ▼

want that old saying, "An iron hand in a velvet glove," because iron is too strong a word, this in case.

There is a tricky line, the thinnest of fine lines, between too much and too little, and that is one of the reasons that there are never that many exceptionally gifted riders in the world at any given time. Yes, we want to have the strength, but, no, we don't want to use that strength. If you figure out how to achieve that, you'll open all sorts of closed doors. This process starts with thinking, "How little can I do, and still get it done?" Or, phrased another way, "Do as much as I have to, but no more than I need to."

_ Causes of Resistance and Disobedience

"This horse won't do what I want." Or, "Why won't my horse do what he's supposed to?"

A question like this gets asked every day. The easy answer is often given as, "Because he's being bad." This is almost always the wrong answer, and it is one of the responses that, more than almost anything, differentiates the bad horsemen and horsewomen from the good ones.

Good horse people will look for real reasons rather than convenient answers. It makes sense, then, to understand the root causes of most "resistance" or "disobedience," because once we know where to look, it sets us up to start to fix the problem. Horses "resist" for four main reasons or combinations of the four. Here they are, in no particular order:

1) Exuberance, or too much energy

2) Ignorance of what is being asked (not well trained)

3) Fear, nervousness, anxiety

4) Pain or discomfort, various levels

Let's take them one at a time, starting with the easiest fix: too much raw energy.

Too Much Energy

Horses aren't designed to sit in tiny stalls 24 hours a day. In a free-roaming situation, horses graze and move and cover ground. Any exuberance is easily burned off by play or by running. Once the excess energy is gotten rid of, the horse goes back to grazing or sleeping.

When humans restrict horses from doing this by keeping them in barns or small paddocks, and then give them lots of high energy feed, it can be like packing gun powder into a canister: light the match and that powder is going to blow.

Add another ingredient: the natural tendencies of the individual horse. Some horses are low-key and phlegmatic. Standing around suits them just fine. But there are some horses who are just bundles of energy, and when a high-octane horse is penned up and not allowed to blow off the excess, he's apt to be hard to ride or drive in a calm way. No big surprise there. So, with the horse that is simply too high, give him more turnout and more work, maybe be careful how much he eats, other than enough hay to keep him at a good weight.

_ The Horse Doesn't Understand

Next, the horse who is being asked something that he doesn't understand. The analogy often used is the person who is being held up by someone who speaks a different language. The robber speaks French. The victim speaks only German. The robber says, "Give me your money or I will shoot you." The victim just stands there because he has no clue what he's being told. So the robber shoots him.

Ridiculous, right? But that happens constantly to horses who are given signals that they fail to understand and are punished for failing to respond to.

Which leads to the next course of "resistance," which is nervousness, anxiety, and fear.

_ Nervousness, Anxiety, and Fear

Horses are just generally a timid species and will normally run to escape danger. So that's something to keep in mind. Now, think of the various reasons that the horse might be nervous about being ridden. He could be very green, not used to being touched, handled, dealt with by a human. He may have been hurt or abused in his past riding or driving. If we go back to our French-speaking robber and our German-speaking victim, this horse may have been asked to perform something that he didn't comprehend and then been punished for not doing it. So now he's scared of people, and can you blame him?

As mentioned, humans do some barbaric things to force horses to obey. They strap them into leverage devices like draw-reins, tight bitting rigs, tight nosebands, sharp bits—all designed to coerce them into obedience. When you are working with a horse who has been abused in any of these ways, why wouldn't this horse be afraid of you? He has been taught to be wary of humans, and the only way to get rid of the anxiety is to prove to him that you are not going to use force.

But don't expect quick results. His fear may be deep-seated, and just because you are nice to him for a day, a week, a month, this may not be long enough to get him to relax. Your only hope is consistent patience and kindness.

_ Pain and Discomfort

Pain causes all sorts of resistance, and pain can range from mildly uncomfortable to agony, and the first key to helping the horse who feels pain is to figure out the cause of the discomfort.

Some causes of pain are more evident than others. When the horse has a hot, swollen girth or saddle sore, you can see it, and if you touch one, he will flinch away from you. But you can't see when your horse has ulcers. Consider: Is his bridle too tight? Does the bit hurt his mouth? Does he have sharp molars that are causing him to eat his cheeks? Is the noseband too tight? Is your riding soft and elastic, or are you coming down too heavily on his back? Do you have soft and sympathetic hands, or are you too strong on the reins? Is your horse shod correctly, or does the footing cause him discomfort? Certainly, if your horse is overtly lame, head bobbing off, you can see it, but there are gradations of unsoundness below the clearly obvious.

One of the biggest "hidden" causes of pain and distress is simple fatigue. If you want to know how much physical exertion can hurt, run up a hill. Or drop down and start firing off push-ups.

Horses seem so much stronger than puny little humans that it's easy to assume they have automatic physical fitness. That's wrong. A horse can only produce what his workload has made him fit enough for. A simple weekend "joy ride" for a human may be far from joyous to a struggling, panting horse. And then, when he

Field Notes
A Tale of Two Horses

— Dapper Dan on his way to placing second in the 1960 GMHA 100-mile. Dan had never been hurt, although he had worked equally hard as a farm horse, but at a far slower pace. It's speed that does the damage—not always, but more often than not. ▼

This is a tale of two horses: one, Dapper Dan, with the cleanest legs in Vermont, and one, Happy Jay, with an old bowed tendon.

This goes straight to that old barn-repair analogy, that a sagging roof is not because of something that first went wrong with the roof, but because there was a weakness down at ground level, and as that got more pronounced, it was like dominoes, bing, bing, bing—from bad to worse.

Take the little chestnut, the half-Quarter horse Dapper Dan, who I rode on the GMHA 100-mile trail ride in 1960. Dapper Dan was a light work horse, and his owner had used him in a team with his brother to rake and ted hay, haul maple sap, and haul wagon loads of manure. All that slow hard work, over many years, had built up in Dan such a rock-hard base of fitness that all I had to do was add some trotting and he was ready to place second in a tough 100-mile

— For an animal as big and strong and fast as a horse, that 1,000-pound body is held up by thin and often vulnerable legs. If the stresses on those legs get too dramatic, the horse can suffer what is called "a breakdown." That's what happened to Happy Jay in a race—a bowed tendon. The tendon healed and he was restarted as a sport horse. ◀

Denny Emerson | *Begin and Begin Again*

124

ride, finishing practically untouched by the effort.

Happy Jay, I was told, was raced hard as a young horse before he had developed any substantial base of fitness or endurance, and after one race, he came in with a blown tendon. Over time, the tendon healed into one of those unsightly "banana-bows." Happy Jay was plenty sound enough for point-to-point races and for eventing, but he was always compromised by an injury that would not have happened if he had been given more chance to get fit first and worked hard after.

Foundation and base-building—so boring and time-consuming for many trainers, to the point where they don't provide enough of it, and who always pays? The horse. ◆

slows down, we hit him with a stick to go faster. Now he is both in pain from the fatigue and he is scared from the punishment. Good job, human!

Stop leaping to the false conclusion, "My horse won't do what I want. Therefore, he is being bad." Your horse is not being bad. He has a reason for his behavior, and your job is to figure out the real reason, or reasons, and start to work on repairing or alleviating the underlying causes.

You will never make a better new beginning with any horse until you learn how to help your horse instead of blaming him.

— Dressage with a Big "D" and with a Small "d"

If I asked 10 dressage experts to define the word "dressage," I might get 17 definitions. Nobody really knows. What they do know is that their way is right. So, as a card-carrying member of the "fools rush in where angels fear to tread" brigade, here are some thoughts.

Little dressage, no capital "d," is a system of horse training. What might differentiate a dressage-based training system from any other system? Good question. So here are some other questions that might help define the answer to that first one.

Is a system of training that relies upon force and subjugation of the horse "dressage-based"? Is a system of training that relies upon such leverage devices as draw-reins, de Gogues, bitting rigs, tie-downs, and crank nosebands "dressage-based"? Is a system of training that relies upon making the horse feel enough pain to give in to bit or leg pressure "dressage-based"? Is a method of training that mainly takes a horse beyond his anxiety threshold "dressage-based"?

If "no" is the right answer to all five of these questions, which I think it should be, then what about these questions?

Is a system of schooling designed to improve a horse's strength and flexibility but without causing undue anxiety and discomfort "dressage-based"? Is a system of training that uses a system of pressures and releases to teach the horse how to respond to various stimuli, while doing so in calm and non-coercive ways, "dressage-based"?

The answer to these last two questions is "yes."

As I discussed earlier, an untrained horse doesn't understand the system that we call "aids," which are basically nonverbal communications, applied with various pressures and releases from the hands, seat, legs, and balance of the rider to various parts of the horse. Just as we teach the young human child in letters, then words, then sentences, then phrases, so we teach the untrained horse to respond in various desired ways to various specific pressures and releases (the "aids").

But there is much more to it. A horse may learn what the human asks, but the horse must also have the physical strength to accomplish the requested task. And the horse must also have the requisite flexibility and

A Blank Slate

A newborn foal is a blank slate in some ways, but not in all ways. Many hereditary qualities are already there, and dealing well with these will be part of the training process.

It starts with handling the foal. Getting the foal used to humans—acceptance of being guided by humans, handled by humans—and while there is often some struggle, there shouldn't be much fighting. By the time the foal is a yearling, he should lead, let you pick up all four hooves, let you gently touch his head, ears, and belly without being scared, those kinds of basics. Then, as the foal gets to be two or three, there should be more acceptance of handling, now including tack, some careful longeing, long-lining, ground-driving, getting used to calmly going into a horse trailer. And if all of this has gone well, the chances are good that when it comes time to mount the young horse, he will just calmly stand still.

Once the youngster accepts a rider, the next logical step is to ride him next to a steady older horse, so he gets used to going places, seeing things, and is relaxed about all of that. Add in quiet application of the most basic aids—go forward,

Some trainers have the almost magical ability to take a little foal like this baby and teach him to lead, stand, pick up each hoof, all with little force or coercion. Horses started like this develop two equally magical qualities—confidence and trust. ▼

Denny Emerson | *Begin and Begin Again*

slow down, stop, stand still, turn right, turn left—until he understands this fundamental work. Aids are basically nonverbal words, applied with pressures and releases, rather than with vocal cords. He learns that certain light pressures, when yielded to, elicit a release of the pressure. He is learning at a level, ideally and in theory, well below his anxiety threshold. We start with basic "words," the way first-graders learn C-A-T, D-O-G, and so forth. Gradually, we add to his vocabulary.

It's as simple as we make it, one step leading to the next. We also know that fatigue is a show-stopper, so we try to do enough walking out, maybe some trotting, to give him some base fitness, and over weeks and months, we carefully build on it.

None of this is rocket science, as they say, but it does involve a few key elements.

Above all else, it takes patience. It takes as long as it takes. Then, an understanding of how to "talk" to a horse through a correct application of the aids. It also requires a willingness to go back a step or two, if something seems confusing to the youngster, and take the time to rebuild. ◆

range of motion to be able to perform. In this way, dressage-based training is a combination of teaching the horse what this pressure means, what that release thanks him for, while simultaneously getting the horse to actually perform the requested movements over enough weeks and months to build the strength and flexibility that permit the horse to do it without too much fatigue or fear.

You can't grind on a horse to get him to improve, but neither can you leave him alone to wander about his meadow. Becoming an athlete requires the expenditure of physical energy. How do we get the horse to do this in a positive way? Now that's the tricky part.

One way to understand this is to equate it with humans in school. Humans begin in kindergarten, then first grade, second grade, and so on. Each grade builds upon what was learned earlier. Most children can't successfully skip grades, and neither should we expect this of the horses that we train.

How "Field Dressage" Helps You Do Everything

Let's talk about "field dressage" and the application of the half-halt, and why it is such a necessary skill to have packed in your toolbox. I read an article once about the use of dressage-based techniques "out in the fields," rather than in a ring, and the importance of basic training for safety, control, balance—in general, "just riding."

In eventing, here is a far-too-familiar sight that we hate to watch: some horse and rider

Falling for Dressage

By Lindle Sutton

I asked my dressage coach, Lindle Sutton, whether she agreed with the premise of this book. This is her response.

– Denny Emerson –

There are many reasons riders who were dedicated to, if not obsessed with, everything horse-related while growing up had to step back from it as a young adult or older. For some, this was fine. For others, that omnipresent hunger always lurked in the shadows.

When the stars realigned, allowing reentry to the horse world, hopefully an acknowledgement of one's options comes with it. Of course there are the obvious parameters of financial and time commitment restrictions.

Fortunately, there is usually an acquired wisdom with age, life experiences, and a sense of a finite timeline that should/could lead to serious thoughts on the accomplishments wanted and the journey to be taken. In youth, many of us jumped onto that hamster wheel that was presented to us.

This re-acquaintance brings with it the freedom to make choices, to find the excitement of getting lost in the woods, the connection that comes with a non-English speaking partner, a new look at sport psychology, attentiveness to mindful horsemanship and/or to choose the trainer and discipline that is right for you, be it to expand your comfort zone or to keep you learning within it.

The world of computers—the internet and social media—offer masses of information such as virtual clinics in many disciplines, symposiums, breed information and associations, statewide associations geared to education and show venues, and of course, time vampires of breathtaking videos of the best of the best doing their thing. So, be free to do YOUR thing!

Below is a brief biography that you may find helpful:

- *I grew up in rural Vermont. I learned how to milk at eight and drive a tractor at 10. I started riding at six under the guidance of my grandfather. That was the start of my lifelong passion for horses.*

- *After college I spent 12 years in formal and constant training. Upon seeing my first dressage trainer, Klaus Albin, ride, it became clear to me that this would be my life's work.*

- *After moving east from Seattle, I took Klaus's advice and worked with the incomparable Karl and Cindy (Sydnor) Mikolka. They were the royalty of the classical foundation of training and the rider's position. But then Karl and Cindy moved away. For the next nine years,*

I worked with Karin Schlüter (Billings) and Robert Dover simultaneously. To this day, I am astounded by their compassion, knowledge, and ability to challenge me to my limit. This was the beginning of my FEI training and showing career.

• *Later I had the good fortune to have brief programs with Rosemarie Springer, Willi Schultheis, and Miguel Ralão Duarte. What I wouldn't do to have that privilege again.*

• *Outside riding and teaching dressage, I study martial arts. After qualifying at the Florida State Championships (silver) in taekwondo, I competed in the National Championships in Atlanta, Georgia, in 1994. I now study tai chi.*

• *I am a member of our town's Conservation Commission, a passionate environmentalist, and the founder of the nonprofit Equestrians-4theEarth.* ◆

"A goal without a plan is just a wish," wrote Antoine de Saint-Exupery. Lindle Sutton was just another of thousands of backyard riding kids, living on a farm near Brattleboro, Vermont. But unlike thousands of backyard riding kids who remain at the basic levels (nothing wrong with that) she wanted more. So Lindle made plans, which led to goals, which led to becoming an upper-level dressage rider, trainer, coach, and teacher. ▲

— In this photo of Core Buff schooling in our ring in Strafford, Vermont, you can see that his forehand is elevated, and his hind legs are sweeping underneath him so that there is a degree of "lift" as well as "push." A technical term for stepping farther under the body mass to create lightness in front is "engagement," another way of saying "to sit and lift." ▲

— Here, on the steeplechase course at the Kentucky Three-Day Event, we see Core Buff in a diametrically opposite profile from the dressage photo. He is flat and elongated, reminiscent of the profile of a racing Greyhound—just what is needed to cover ground in a sweeping gallop stride. ▼

are wing-dinging along, coming to a solid fence, flat, unbalanced, hocks trailing, body low—and just when a good rider would sit up a bit, take a little half-halt, or two, or three, the inexperienced rider, somehow thinking that speed will get the horse to the other side, leans forward and goes faster. That's a train wreck waiting to happen, but most of the time, with the rider totally unaware that the wrong technique is being applied, the pair blunder over without falling.

If you look at the two photos on this page of the Thoroughbred stallion Core Buff, one schooling in an arena, the other on steeplechase at Rolex, it is plain to see how easily I could adjust his canter stride in the first photo, and what a lot more it would take to set him up—"spring load" his hocks—in the second photo.

Jack Le Goff used to have a joke about that (complete with French accent): "My horse is galloping flat and fast toward the big ditch and wall, all strung out. I pick up the telephone to dial the horse, but…there is no answer."

Don't expect the horse to answer the phone in the excitement and adrenaline rush of cross-country if he hasn't had plenty of schooling while being ridden on the flat. We have to install those conditioned reflexes of accepting the half-halt in situations where he can learn them, so when we truly need them, they are there. And even then, we may need more bit with some horses—not as substitutes for training, but because some horses are simply more aggressive and on-going than others.

The worst wrecks are rotational falls, and coming screaming along on the forehand and not listening to that phone ringing (accepting the half-halt) is not a great way to avoid such things.

Dressage out in the wide-open spaces is actually more key than in the confines of a 20-by-60-meter rectangle, when we analyze the physics of trajectory and thrust and balance.

— Two Key Steps

Let's discuss the two ever-so-fundamental but interlocking methods to create and produce sound, healthy, and rideable horses—the consistent application of hacking out and basic flatwork—and why and how they augment one another so well.

Take a horse, human, dog, any species, really, and four to five days a week, have that person, dog, or horse go for an active hike of at least an hour, and do this for months. What will you see? You'll see the creation of muscle tone, a general look of healthy fitness, as compared to that same entity spending day after day sitting. This is simple fact, and it is simple to do. All it requires is the place to ride or walk and the willingness to do it.

Field Notes

Closing Up the Canter

The idea of "closing up" the canter stride, so that the horse is asked for a bit more "sit and lift," is akin to that moment in doing a push-up when your sternum is touching the ground, your arms are bent, and you are about to exert enough force to come up. But the horse will do it mainly from behind, and that, mainly from being engaged, so it's a good idea to have some sort of definition of what "engaged" means.

Knowing how dressage fans love to bicker, squabble, and stew over minutiae, I hesitate to throw out any working definition, but you have to start with something, so here's one I wrote down from a French

—Let's face facts. For hundreds of years, Thoroughbreds have been bred for one reason: to drop down, open up, and run faster than the other horses in the race. So to ask a former racehorse like Tense here, who raced 34 times, to engage and lift rather than to reach and propel, is going counter to both his breeding and his physical structure. But little by little he's getting the idea, and as his strength increases, it gets easier for him, and as it gets easier, he becomes more willing to try. But it can't be rushed. ▼

Denny Emerson | *Begin and Begin Again*

translation years ago: "Engagement: The act of flexing the hocks and stifles, thereby bringing the hind legs more fully under the center of the horse's mass, planting those legs, and lifting."

Engagement is akin to power lifting, and it is not easy or comfortable, as any gym rat knows, so it's important to get a glimmer, ease off, come again, get a sense of lift, back off. Over a period of weeks, barring injury or accident, it will get easier. Over months, still more so. But any time we allow ourselves the luxury of frustration to the point where we start to grind and demand, we are playing with fire. If we make the horse start to fear and hate the work, it can start a downward spiral, and this is much easier to prevent than it is to repair.

There is a fine line—too little effort, not much gain. Too much pain, the horse gets demoralized. It is a big reason to take lessons from someone who can safely monitor the difference. ◆

It's not extreme, it's not fast or particularly rigorous, but it gets its effectiveness through consistency. Go try this yourself, to get a taste. Go walk like you mean it for as much time as it takes you to feel that you have done something. If you have been sedentary, you may feel it in 5 to 10 minutes. Others might easily hike for a couple of hours.

But what will happen, if you keep it up, day by day, week by week, month by month, is a general hardening of all sorts of body parts, muscles, tendons, ligaments, bones, heart, wind.

Now, add weight-lifting, which in riding will be basic flatwork, because we will begin to ask the horse for engagement. Engagement is essentially getting the horse to sit down and lift his own weight (see more in the sidebar). If you don't already know how to get a horse to do this correctly, consider taking lessons.

Those are the basics on a silver platter: walking and some trotting out on the trails for general overall strength and fitness, to which we add weight-lifting two to three days a week for more strength and flexibility.

You know one big problem? It is actually too simple, and many riders don't grasp how basic this type of program actually is so they don't do it, or if they do, they are erratic about it. This doesn't take enormous skill, but it does take both basic dressage proficiency, which we can learn, plus the willingness to be unrelentingly consistent, and that right there is the hardest part.

Releasing the Inner Jungle Cat

Lots of horses have two to three gradations of trot: a little chop-chop trot, an okay trot, and a swinging trot where the back and neck get involved in the process, and the ordinary becomes slinky and slithery, transforming the plain movement into something special. Not all horses have the hidden fifth gear, and even for

those horses that do, it often takes an equally slithery rider to find and release it.

"Dressage" with a capital D makes many riders haul out their most earnest selves. "I must do this well," thinks the rider, and tries so hard not to make mistakes that tension and stiffness creep in. Horses don't move like stalking panthers for tight riders. But watch riders who are themselves like jungle cats or writhing snakes. Everything is flexible, elastic, flowing—hips, knees, elbows, wrists, fingers—and their way of "melting" into the body of the horse creates a counter melt in the way the horse moves. Some of this is physical elasticity, but the most fundamental elastic component is the flexibility of the mind and emotions, because when the emotions are earnest and rigid, don't expect that physical snake-like writhing and cat-like slink from your horse or from yourself.

Let go of the thoughts in your busy head so you can feel the release in your riding body, to be one with the horses you ride. You have to be that strange combination of Cowboy Clem, soft and relaxed and smooth and unconcerned, along with Dressage Doug, balanced, tall, elegant, and precise. This is not an easy goal, which is why so few of us can pull it off, but it's a worthy vision to strive for. ◈ ◈ ◆

BEGIN

to Try the Impossible

Riding in the dark changes the whole equation. It's ever so much slower, and the rock with your name on it becomes invisible, too. Unless I'm lost or it's raining, I love riding at night.

8

It is a cliché that the best-case scenario is when someone's work is the same as what one does for pleasure. Robert Frost describes it this way in the poem "Two Tramps in Mud Time":

But yield who will to their separation,
My object in living is to unite
My avocation and my vocation
As my two eyes make one in sight.

When I got into the saddle on Victor Dakin the morning of September 14, 1974, about to set out onto the hugely daunting 17-mile cross-country day of roads and tracks, steeplechase, and cross-country jumping that was formerly the heart of the World Three-Day Event Championships in Burghley, England, I did not then know that what happened that day—my success or failure—would set the direction for the rest of my professional life. I was 33 and had been a school teacher and a real estate broker, working to support my riding passion. By being able to have a clear round, I was able to contribute to our United States Equestrian Team's gold medal. My teammates were Bruce Davidson riding Irish Cap, Mike Plumb and Good Mixture, and Don Sachey and Plain Sailing. That gold medal opened the door for me to train horses and instruct riders. It was the classic pivotal moment.

This article, which appeared in *The USCTA News* and is reprinted with permission from *Eventing USA*, is a fence-by-fence account of what happened that day:

_ A Team Gold Medal Winner Rides the Endurance Test

Denny Emerson has been competing for the past eight years. A self-made rider until he was chosen by Jack Le Goff to join the Three-Day Squad this spring, he is part of the very backbone of eventing in this country. In between teaching school, and now as a real estate broker from the "Blue Hills of Vermont" (a quote by Princess Anne—see "The Glitter of Gold"), Denny has been a supporter of and a competitor in this sport since its budding days.

With Victor Dakin, his 10-year-old half-bred gelding, Denny turned in one of the three clear cross-country rounds which contributed toward the winning of the team gold medal. Neither horse nor rider had ever competed internationally before going to England.

Here Denny gives us his reactions to eventing at this level for the first time, and then takes us through the Endurance Phase and over every obstacle of the bold and sweeping Burghley course:

— Fifi Coles

Two of the big differences I noticed between eventing in the United States and England are the size of the field of entries and the speeds at which the British compete. Where we would have a field of 60 entries at an event in both the Preliminary and Intermediate Division combined, the British would have over 260 horses!

To win an event in England you must really go fast. Their Novice Division, which is comparable to our Preliminary Division, is the lowest recognized level offered in England. At this level their required speed for cross-country is 575 meters per minute (mpm), compared to our 520. At the Intermediate and Advanced Levels, the speed is 600 mpm, faster than that of international competition, which is 570 mpm. The British really chase horses, and except at the high levels, you see some wild riding. They bring their young horses along quickly. A horse is quite likely to start at Novice this year and compete at Advanced the next.

In England the courses vary tremendously, as they do in the United States. I had thought that all English courses would be beautiful. Some were, like Sheila Willcox's and Osberton, but some were not. They have the same sort of problems we have here: too-small rails, too-sharp turns, and bad footing. But the big events are simply spectacular!

Burghley has the most ideal setting imaginable, rolling countryside, beautiful turf, and wide-open vistas. The turns are big and sweeping and the rider can see the obstacles from a long way away. It is ideal for galloping.

_ The Burghley Course

There is no doubt about it, the Burghley cross-country course was massive, and nothing that I've done in the United States or Canada prepared me psychologically to jump anything that big. This course never let up on you from the third fence on. It kept hitting you with questions. At one obstacle you might be asked to jump out into space and then at the next to take back at an 18-foot combination, and next sail over a 6½-feet wide, almost 4-feet high oxer. The British riders compete at Badminton and Burghley every year and are well-accustomed to the scope of a course like this. Now, having done it, and the dragon's teeth having been pulled a little, it doesn't seem that bad.

This was a very fair course, however. You could get at every fence. There were some alternative fences that asked questions.

Field Notes
Jumping Competitions

_ A ritual as old as the sport of three-day eventing is walking the cross-country course on foot, often multiple times, to learn where you are going, and to plan your approach and your strategy for each jump. This group of course walkers was at Hitching Post Farm in Royalton, Vermont. ▼

There's a ritual that all of us who compete in any sort of jumping competition know well.

Whether it's a show-jumping course in an arena, a cross-country course, or the four miles of the Maryland Hunt Cup, we walk them on foot before we ride over them.

We do this for many reasons, and the most basic one is to know where we are going so we don't go off course, get lost, lose our way.

Then there are 101 technical aspects: At what angle should I approach this downhill combination? Should I plan on five or six strides between fences seven and eight? Is the two-stride distance in 4A to 4B going to ride short, long, or easy? Where can I make time, where do I need to slow down because of accuracy requirements? Can I roll

Denny Emerson | *Begin and Begin Again*

back inside the sailboat oxer to save time getting to number 8? And so on.

In eventing, which takes you over big cross-country courses, many riders walk it four times—the first for that initial look, the second, for a careful fence-by-fence analysis, usually with a coach or friends. The third, a solitary walk, riding it in your head, imagining how it will feel on a galloping horse. And, sometimes, over the big ones, that early morning last lone walk, in the fog of the actual day, nervous, intensely focused. "I am going to jump this right here."

Learn to do this by doing this. Get past the point of needing a coach to tell you every little detail. Yes, have and use a coach, but remember: you and your horse are all alone out there. Get used to relying on each other, because ultimately, you are all he's got, and he is all you've got. ◆

The difficult ones were the obstacles where the ground gave way in front of the fence and where there was an impressive drop on the far side. There was never an easy choice. No matter where you jumped it, you had to stand back and fly out over the rails. If you didn't, you went down or stopped. You really had to ride forward.

_ On Course!

Phase A: The roads and tracks are a little over 6 kilometers, and I must do 1 kilometer every four minutes. I also want to do about one minute at about 400 mpm in order to do what Jack says—"put them on their legs a bit"—get them ready to gallop. So we start out through the deer park next to the start of cross-country and head through a big stone gate into some woods through some rather rocky footing, to the top of a hill. After about 2 kilometers we come onto some good footing on a nice long track through the woods. Victor is nice and relaxed so I pick up my canter here, which puts me quite a bit ahead of my time.

We come to some dirt roads next to the Bull Pens, No. 16 and 17. I can see the huge crowds all over the cross-country course. I thought I might be nervous, but fortunately I don't seem to get very much so anymore. Looking at my watch again, I see I am now about two minutes early reaching the box at steeplechase, so we just walk around and wait. Fortunately, Victor isn't nervous and doesn't pull a "Plain Sailing," who sometimes rears in the starting gate. He's quite good and relaxed, which is a pleasant change from one of our earlier events, Osberton, where he was quite bad. The loudspeakers really upset him there.

Steeplechase: The 2-mile course is situated on the Burghley golf course. In order not to incur penalty points we must finish in five minutes 30 seconds. The idea is to check my watch at the first lap to see if I have done it in two minutes 45 seconds. After listening to the countdown, we are off. It's a long-looking mile ahead and we must go around twice. Victor is galloping and jumping well, and checking my watch, I see that we are just about on the nose at 2:45. He is a little bit of an unknown quantity, as he has never done a big three-day event like this before. This is the first 2-mile steeplechase he has ever done.

When you are riding on the Team, each person has specific orders. My orders with Victor were to feel him out, see how much he had, and most important—get around clear. You have four people going, and if you can get the first two around clear, or with not too much trouble, then the coach, Jack Le Goff, is in a better position to send the other two riders on a bit and go for better time. When Victor started to get tired on the second lap, I took back, because I wanted to be sure I had enough horse left for the cross-country course.

Phase C: The land is flat with good footing, the temperature is not too hot. Now that the steeplechase is finished, I want to give Victor a breather. The best way to do this is to get off and walk beside him. As part of our training we must jog at least a mile each day so that I'm ready to jog beside him if need be. We walk along this way for about three minutes so that he can recover. I will have to catch up and be on my correct time by the middle of roads and tracks by cantering. I pop back in the saddle and Victor falls into a nice swinging rhythm at the trot, and shortly we pick up a canter to make up for the walk earlier.

He has come back quickly after our walk. I thought he was really tired after steeplechase. Also I think he is a trifle overweight. Jack realized about two weeks ago that Victor was slightly heavier than he would have liked, but you can't do much galloping then because you stand a chance of hurting him. Victor is sort of an unknown quantity; he's a non-Thoroughbred and has never done anything quite like this before. He hasn't been at the Team very long, either. The time goes by faster than I thought it would and we are soon on our way to the box for the vet check and the start of Phase D.

Phase D: Jack is in the box where I am headed for the vet check before the start of the cross-country. He tells me what the other riders have done and how the Team stands. He says that Don has had a fall on Plain Sailing, and Beth Perkins on Furtive has gone clean. Beth's score doesn't count for the Team because she is competing as an individual. This makes a difference, as the individual can go on a bit and do their thing, but the Team rider must follow a specific order, which will benefit the Team as a whole. With Victor, the main thing is to get around the course clear, and not too slowly. The 10 minutes in the box flies by awfully quickly. And before I know it, I'm back up in the saddle for the countdown. We are off again as Victor starts on the fourteenth mile of the endurance phase. We gallop on down to the first fence, which is a big wagon with a log—not very high. I want to get Victor going forward and jumping "already-going-forward" or what the British call "attacking the fences." He jumps it well and nicely in balance. We proceed on down a long lane lined with people on both sides, and then cross a road and press on down to a wooden wall. This is a straightforward fence, a nice warm-up, and we are over it easily.

The next fence is a chair-type obstacle, very big and very wide with maximum spread. It was constructed of wooden slats that made me think that a horse, if he chose to bank it, could easily get a leg down through the slats. This fence starts to set the tone of the course—big fences with big spreads. We drift up so that we get a fairly straight shot at it, and Victor jumps it out of a forward galloping stride.

Galloping along over the beautiful turf lanes, which are formed by ropes holding back the crowds, I can see fence No. 4 just ahead. We swing around the left and then back to the right for a straight approach to the easy alternative, which is the single rails. We lose a little time doing this, but it's not worth risking anything.

We continue on, hardly noticing the crowds, which I was told later were about 50,000 on the cross-country. We are heading down a little hill and just ahead lies the Double Coffin. After the first stockade fence, the ground drops down and there are two ditches and then a very steep bank before the last fence. Princess Anne had a stop here at the out as Goodwill got under it and couldn't get out.

I don't want Victor to be able to stop, coming into the first element by looking over it, so I keep his head up, sit up a bit and keep my lower legs well on him. As we land, I look up at the escape hatch, the "out," at the top of the hill. I don't worry what he does over the two ditches—he's very agile—I just ride for the "out" and he runs up the bank and pops out over the top.

Then we swing left-handed, and we run down to the next fence, which has a little bank in front of it. He is so handy that he jumps up onto this bank and is up and over the fence and we are away again.

Driving Aids: A Discussion

Many years ago, I was told that there are only three real driving aids that can be employed on the approach to a fence: the stick, the cluck, and the leg. (And, no, prayer is not a fourth.)

There are a couple of others that "feel" like driving aids, the worst of which is that tendency we all have to "push" with our upper bodies, an instinctive move that I believe is related to how in most other sports, running, skating, the first thing we do is to lean forward.

Think about how, in track, for sprint races, they actually line up already in a leaning position. So when a rider feels the need to "help" make the horse go, what is more instinctive than to lean? But try this: Sit on your horse, and suddenly lean forward. Does he sprint away? No. Does he walk away? Not usually. He may flick his ears back as if to say, "What is this silly thing up to?" but that's about it.

— Abby Emerson on Roxy. ▼

So write this down: "Throwing my upper body is NOT a driving aid."

Another false driving aid is sort of contorting around, pushing with the seat. This has minimal effect. And the cluck only works if the horse has learned to associate the cluck with the spur or the stick, which leaves only two primary driving aids, the most dramatic of which is a smack with a stick. But what is the big problem with this one? You have to take one hand off the reins to use it. And at the last minute in front of a jump, that can open the door to a run-out. Now we come to the leg. But again, this gets tricky.

Try this: Sit on your horse at a standstill. Now, squeeze with your knees only, as hard as you can. You will be lucky to elicit an ear flick. Try again, with just your upper calf. He might move, but he probably won't.

Now, relax your knees a bit, and close your lower leg against his hair, down by the little ridge on your boot called the spur mount. Off he will usually go.

So when your instructor is having a writhing, mouth-frothing fit, screaming at you, "LEEEG! Use MORE LEG!" and your horse isn't going anywhere, you are probably using the wrong part of your leg.

There is another element at play here, as shown in the two photos, one of my 11-year-old granddaughter Abby Emerson on Roxie, the other of my former barn manager Daryl Kinney on Monte Carlo. Abby doesn't have any leg (she's tiny) but Roxie goes anyway. Why? Training. Roxie and Monte have both been trained to see a fence and to go and jump it. The difference is that Daryl has the tools to fix things if she feels Monte backing off, while Abby doesn't yet have them.

So many riders lack leg aids that they can apply when needed, because they either lack the

Daryl Kinney on Monte Carlo. ▼

strength, the proper technique, or they lack both.

A word to the wise: If you can't apply the driving aids correctly, especially that crucial lower-leg driving aid, go fix it before you need it. Why go through life with such a huge missing piece in your arsenal of skills, when it can be learned? ◆

On the course-walk, I felt that this fence would set a tone, as it requires the bold yet clever horse. It consists of sloping rails out of a poor approach. Coming down a little hill, it flattens out with only about one stride and then you have to shoot forward. Victor likes to come down to his fences and check himself, then jump. On this kind of fence you can't do this. So I chase Victor into it, and he answers by jumping boldly over it, and up onto the bank on the far side.

The Log Pile is another big fence, so I decide this is the moment to test him on this kind of fence. I don't check him at all except to remind him that the fence is coming up, and he sails over it in fine style. Now, I start to think I'm going to have a good round as he is jumping really boldly. It's a little early to think this, I suppose, but that's the feeling I have. My biggest worry is that he might run out of gas.

Galloping on, we are now approaching the Stockade. This is a drop onto the road. Well, he doesn't hesitate and pops over it, down the bank onto the road and up the bank on the other side. He really has lots of spring.

Now we head down a long hill and swing to the right. I don't check him much at all, just sort of set him. Victor always checks himself; he comes into this fence, does a quick check, and clears the simple straightforward gate with no problem.

We wind up a long hill toward the Dairy Farm Rails. At this point, I want to see how much horse I have left. This is what Jack calls "listening to the motor." So, I ask Victor to go forward, which he does. But he does not "spurt" forward, so I know I have to back off a bit. There is still a long way to go, and I want to make sure I will have enough horse to finish with. We are about a third of the way around the course and have gone over 14 miles. We still have almost 3 miles to go. Well, we head up to the Rails, which has a very steep approach, and he pops up and out over it very handily.

Now we swing left. This is one of the fences that I have been worried about. It consists of a big bank that then slopes down with a big fence out in front of it, plus a 6-foot drop. Jack had told us to ride that fence as though there was no bank there, and when you are in the air, to sit back a bit, so that the horse can get his landing gear down. As we approach it, I can feel Victor doing his "Victor Dakin shuffle." As I said, he likes to come to a fence and shift his feet, which gives him time to have a look at it, and then go. So I reach back and go to the bat, which scares the "shuffle" out of him. Well, he just sails out into space like a rocket and lands just fine. What a nifty horse! I had heard, before starting the cross-country, that several horses had had problems at this fence.

I'm feeling great as we approach the big Lamb Creep. We head on at the fence, and sure enough, Victor banks it. He pops his feet down behind, just as I figured he might, as he did this same thing at Ledyard last year. Fortunately, he never seems to slip doing it—he's exceptionally clever with his feet.

The land is generally quite flat, and I'm not pressing him. I'd say we are galloping at about 520 to 530 mpm. I'm still concerned with having enough horse left to finish. The Sleeper table is another one of the big oxers that this course features. It rides well for Victor. At these big oxers, Victor doesn't do his "shuffle," because this is the kind of fence that allows him to see what's required. He only does it when he cannot quite see what's there. He has a great regard for his own well-being and doesn't like to hit a fence one bit. In a three-day horse, this is a trait that you have to stifle a bit.

Well, before I know it we are over the Hayrack, which is quite straightforward. He has jumped it very nicely. Now I start thinking of my approach to the next combination.

We run down toward the Bull Pens, which is sort of a maze. We decided earlier that we would do this as

_ Fences like this maximum dimension slanting table are actually easier for horses to jump than smaller jumps that are made of "bits and pieces" because the horse can see exactly what the job requires. I brought Victor Dakin at a fast gallop right dead center, and he coiled and unloaded, the closest feeling that riders get to some big bird of prey taking flight. ▼

Field Notes
The Hidden Part of Jumping

_ When a canter has too much impulsion, the horse tends to go forward and down. The rider can lengthen the stride, but he can't easily shorten it. When a horse is asked to lift and hold a more upright balance, and we ask too strongly for balance, the impulsion gets snuffed out. Now we can shorten but not easily lengthen. The ideal is to create a canter where impulsion and balance are precisely meshed, far easier to talk about than to do. Here I am playing with the canter with Atti a couple of years ago. I'm first letting her lengthen as shown, then bringing her back into balance. ▼

What is the "hidden" part of a great jumping effort? Well, it isn't how the rider looks in terms of her own form in the air. We can see that. And it isn't what the horse's form looks like in the air. We can see that. And it isn't whether or not she gets her horse to good takeoff distances. We can see that too. So what is it that is much harder to see?

It is the rider's "sense of canter," her ability to create just the right balance between impulsion and balance, which will give her the option of instantly going forward or instantly shortening, whatever she needs, when she needs it, and without a lot of struggle to get it. A great show-jumping rider was described in these words: "Her body is a tuning fork for the right canter."

This needs to be talked about more in most jumping lessons, because although it's harder to see, it is a huge part of the equation. ◆

Denny Emerson | *Begin and Begin Again*

three separate fences, instead of trying to jump the corner to save time, which is very risky indeed. So we come down to a trot, turn right, jump in, stop, turn left, jump out, turn right, and jump out again. All six of our horses did it this way and all six of them went through fine. The horses that tried the corner, except for one, quit or ran out, so it was the right decision. Victor hits the "out" because, as we turn right, I chase Victor to the bottom of the "out." This is a mistake. He isn't able to set himself up as he usually does, and he hits the fence in front and pecks on landing but is okay.

There is quite a dip in front of the Wall, and the Bank runs right up after it. The Wall rides very well, as Victor is very nimble and probably has an easier time than some of the big horses.

We press on and make a U-turn into the Steps Down and Up. This is Victor's cup of tea—his footwork is quick and agile and he just jumps in, takes a stride, jumps down, takes a stride at the bottom, jumps up and takes a stride out over the rails. He seems to know where he is every second.

Running on, we cross a road and head into the Hanging Log, which is maximum height and could give a tired horse a problem. Fortunately, we sail over it and I start thinking about the Birch Fence coming up next. This is a big fence, indeed, being 4 feet 5 inches in height and 9 feet at the bottom. Well, "ole Victor" banks it, pops his feet down on it, and keeps right on going. At this point the engine is still running well; I'm not chasing him, but trying to keep him in a rhythm. I'm beginning to think we have a good chance to go clear, barring any accidents. He is jumping everything as though he really means it.

The water in the Troughs is recirculated and squirts into each side through a little spout. None of the horses seem to take any notice of this. Victor jumps it in good form. Now I start to think seriously about the next fence that is coming up. It is one of the more difficult ones on the course.

The Waterloo Rails turned out to be well-named, as it was, or almost was, the Waterloo for several horses. This is another one of those bank alternatives that slopes off before the fence with an enormous drop afterward. The bank is all lumpy and uneven. We had decided to take the longer approach around to the left.

I knew Victor would have to forget his "shuffle" and stand off and jump, which happily for me he does and doesn't catch a leg. It seems a long way down. (We would have dinner with the fence judge later that evening, and he'd say Victor was one of the very few horses who didn't hit this fence front or behind.) Riding on down around the edge of some small woods, we turn right into the water, which, if you choose to lose time, you could just jog onto. Victor gallops on down to it and steps in the far side. We are off again.

This combination is a good one for Victor, as it is only 18 feet between the wall and the bank. He jumps in, takes a quick stride and is out. Plain Sailing unfortunately had a little problem by jumping in too big.

Moving on, we come to a good long hill that leads down into the Trout Hatchery. This isn't the "bugaboo" they say it is for nothing! You come down a long hill, the horses are tired, and it's near home. There is a funny little mound that you ride up onto, and then there is a steep slope. It's muddy and you are jumping into the water. The rails stand straight at you, and the horse can see straight through. The crowds are everywhere! I want Victor to jump off the bank, not bury himself under the fence. Also, you can't come in too fast, otherwise the horse might fall on landing in the water. We come in slowly but well in hand. Victor does stand off and land in the water. I think he catches a hind leg on the way down, but all is well, and he splashes through the water and pops out over the log. Princess Anne almost came off here. There were several spectacular falls from horses getting buried under the fence and then going from there.

Moving on up the hill, we head for the Zigzag Rails. This, like the Dairy Drop earlier, is another fence that I am concerned about. It consists of a big ditch with a zigzag over it, with rails 3 feet 11 inches. The approach is downhill into it, at an angle with a big ditch to jump plus an "up" bank on the far side. So it has height, spread downhill, and angle near the end over the course.

— This little gold medal has sat in its small maroon box in my desk for about 47 years. When Prince Philip handed it to me in 1974, he said, "Well done, boys," as he went down the line giving one to Bruce Davidson, to Mike Plumb, to me, and to Don Sachey. I've never displayed trophies the way I guess some do. It's nice to have, but I'm not going to build some shrine to the past when I have other horses waiting to be ridden right now. ◀ ▼

This is the kind of fence you must ride right on down to without checking. If you start looking and checking, you are inviting a stop or a fall. We had determined a specific line, and around the corner we come. We pick our line, I steady him, and he stands off and jumps it very well. Victor really is great.

At this point, although I haven't been pressing on too much, I fortunately have some horse left. There is still that big third-to-last fence to go. Also quite a good gallop on down to the next fence—slightly down-hill. The Birch is big, which is good, as it sets Victor up again and gets him jumping something that stands up in front of him—in preparation for the next fence, which is impressive.

Victor has gone almost 17 miles now, as we head toward fence No. 30. This obstacle is large with maximum height and a 6-foot 6-inch spread. It's built out of solid big poles, yet it's airy. Coming across this long field, as we are about 20 strides out, I set him up a bit by taking a little more hold of him and drive him into my hand. He bounds over it.

It could be a bit premature, but I now feel we are home, as the next fence is a straightforward Trakehner, which should be no problem, but then, you never know. This often is where the problems arise when you get too confident. Anyway, we gallop straight on at it and Victor really flies over it. Later I heard this is where Columbus, ridden by Mark Phillips, pulled his Achilles tendon when he dragged a hind leg over the log. He was withdrawn after cross-country, which was a real shame as he was standing in first place.

Up one little hill, there is not too much of a gallop into the Raleigh Chopper. I never thought a "guillotine" could look so good. He sails on over it, and we run on to the finish line. Victor has some engine left but not a whole lot.

We have time penalties, but the most important thing is that Victor went clear and has been able to handle a course of this magnitude. He's a super little horse.

And the following day our American team won the gold medal.

_ 100 Miles, Here We Come

Going from eventing back to distance riding was not something I'd planned. It happened as the result of a random conversation I had with Lana Wright at the 1998 Fair Hill, Maryland, three-day event.

Way back in 1956, I had met Lana at the Woodstock Inn Stables, when, as kids, we were both riding in the GMHA (Green Mountain Horse Association) 100-Mile Trail Ride in South Woodstock, Vermont.

Later, in 1964, Lana became the first woman to ride in an Olympic three-day event, as part of the silver medal USET squad in Japan. Prior to that, the military

officers who basically ran the sport of eventing had decreed that women were not tough enough to compete on an equal basis with men. But that's a tale for another time.

At any rate, I knew that Lana had taken up a new sport, endurance riding, and I casually asked her how that was going. We were on a hillside overlooking a part of the cross-country course, and I remember that Lana mentioned that she was planning to ride one of her Arabians in a 100-mile race somewhere south of our farm in Southern Pines, North Carolina, and the ride would be later that fall, around Thanksgiving. "I have an extra horse," she said, "a little Arabian who finished the Tevis Cup. Would you like to ride him?"

"Sure," I said, and then basically forgot all about our brief conversation. It came as something of a rude shock when, about two months later, I got an email from Lana, "Will be stopping at your farm in three days to pick you up for our ride in Bethune, South Carolina. Have Zion ready to go. Hope you are ready too."

I didn't even know what "ready" meant. I had never done a ride of 100 miles in a 24-hour period, and the last time I had even ridden 40 miles in a day was probably when I rode Bien Venue in the 1965 GMHA 100-Mile, a three-day ride of 40, 40, and 20 miles, and that was 33 years earlier.

But, as they say, "in for a penny, in for a pound." Too late to back out now.

Zion turned out to be a tiny 14.1 Arabian gelding; I am an inch over 6 feet tall. I took one look at him as he walked off the trailer and thought that there was no conceivable way that I could ride this little guy down the road, never mind 100 miles.

But again, I should have thought about that before I agreed to do it. So I climbed aboard, and miracle of miracles, Zion didn't ride like a little horse. I didn't feel unbalanced or top heavy, so I had a glimmer of hope about what was to come.

_ "A Field Full of Rabid Field Mice"

We drove down to Bethune ("Home of the Chicken Strut," said the sign at the town's entrance) and Lana helped me through the unfamiliar vetting-in process.

Before daylight the next morning, a chilly, drizzly day, we were up—feeding, tacking up, and walking and trotting before the start.

If you have never witnessed the start of a 100-mile race, this description that I heard sums it up pretty well: "It looks like a field full of rabid field mice." Lots of hyper Arabians, heads and tails high, spooking, dancing, pent up, ready to rock and roll.

It wasn't too bad for about the first 30 miles or so. I wasn't anywhere fit enough, but the first few hours were tolerable.

Bethune has thousands of acres of cotton fields, interspersed with wooded trails. It's pretty flat, so the horses didn't have to struggle the way they did on the hilly GMHA rides of my youth. But, inevitably, my lack of having put in the long training hours, added to the fact that at the age of 58, I wasn't a kid anymore, began to create the first symptoms of chafes and aches. Here's the deal: you relentlessly trot. And trot. By the hour. Then trot some more, up, down, up, down, mile after mile.

First my back felt it. Then my shoulders, then legs, feet, ankles, and pretty soon there was no part of my body that didn't hurt. And we still had 50 miles to go.

And then, joy of joys, it started to rain a steady, cold rain. And I already had a cold and should have been wrapped in a blanket on a couch watching a football game!

Starting Over: Stories from Re-Riders

Ashley Tomaszewski

As a child, I was terrified of animals, even to the point that I would avoid going to the park because of the squirrels. Hearing that horses were therapeutic and had a calming effect on people, my loving mother shipped me off to horse camp for a week. I may have cried the first few days, but by the end of the week, I came home with a pet rabbit from the petting zoo and was signed up for another week of camp.

Fast-forward 25 years and I am now engaged to a large-animal veterinarian, just completed my first 75-mile ride, and am planning on competing in the Tevis Cup endurance race this year. ◆

I remember that I was riding somewhere through thick woods, pitch black, except for little glow sticks in pouring rain. We were sort of lost, and it was after midnight, and we still had 12 miles to go. I made a classic mistake, one that you do not make when you are riding with seasoned endurance riders. I whined.

"Well, the bloom is off this rose," I said.

One of my two riding companions responded, "Well, they wouldn't call it endurance if it wasn't hard."

The other was even less sympathetic. She said, "You know, Denny, the biggest compliment you can pay an endurance rider is to call him a boiled owl (the toughest thing to eat in the Maine woods), and you obviously are not one."

We finished about two hours later, and by the next morning, I decided that one day of misery was not enough. I wanted to do more.

I've never figured out why, really, but whenever there's been some riding challenge that I somewhat doubt I might be able to do, like after I saw my first three-day event in 1961, it makes me want to try to prove otherwise. And so began the renewal of my distance riding career.

Although the term "bucket list" wouldn't come into popular parlance for decades, I am pretty sure that I put riding in the Tevis Cup in my bucket back in the late 1950s.

As the decades slipped by, my chances of actually achieving that goal became increasingly slim, while the mythic proportions of the challenge grew stronger. But when I rode little Zion in my first 100-mile endurance ride in 1998, and I began to get involved in that new sport, I began to view the Tevis as an actual possibility.

When I bought Rett Butler in California (a horse who'd already completed that ride) and started to

Denny Emerson | *Begin and Begin Again*

156

compete in some endurance rides on my new horse, the bucket-list item had changed from a dream into an actual goal. Not, however, an easy goal, and my first try, in 2003, saw us get about halfway through the ride, when a stone bruise stopped us from finishing.

The next year, 2004, coincided with the fiftieth running of that ride, and the following story (reprinted with permission from *Practical Horseman* magazine) describes what it was like. It is my first-hand account of my successful completion of the 2004 Tevis Cup endurance race.

_ The Tevis Cup, 2004: Like Riding a Miracle

High in the wild and lonely Sierra Nevada mountains, close to the spot where the Donner party infamously perished in the snow 150 years ago, my alarm starts its insistent beeping at 3:45 a.m. It needn't have bothered. I'm already awake, and have been off and on all night, in my tent under the huge ponderosa pines at Robie Park.

Now, as I struggle into my riding clothes without getting out of my sleeping bag—it's cold at 7,200 feet, even on July 31—I can hear the huge camp beginning to stir to life: 250 endurance horses, 250 riders in varying states of nervous tension, dozens of veterinarians, ride officials, and several hundred rider support personnel ("crew" in endurance terminology) are beginning the endless day that will become the fiftieth

_ When I hold them in my hand, a gold medal like the one handed to me by Britain's Prince Philip (see p. 153) or a buckle like the one I was awarded for completing the Tevis Cup, they are just small metal objects. The gold medal has on the obverse side a bas relief mini-sculpture of a mounted Saint George with a spear, stabbing a dragon. On the reverse side, these words in French, *"Championnat Monde Complet 1974."* The Tevis buckle has a silver base, with a golden image of a galloping horse and rider, and the words "100 Miles, One Day" followed by "Western States Trail Ride." The Tevis Cup promoters like to say, "More people have stood on the summit of Mount Everest than have completed the Tevis ride." I don't know whether that's actually true, and I am certain that it's a great deal harder to summit Everest than to ride the Tevis, but even so, getting that first Tevis Cup Completion buckle is a big deal among endurance riders. It's not the objects—the medal or the buckle—but the fruition of the struggle that they represent that creates the mystique: the two hardest things I ever did on the back of two incredible and generous horses, Victor Dakin and Rett Butler. ▲

running of the Tevis Cup Western States Trail Ride, the oldest, most famous, and most arduous 100-mile horse race in the world.

I hope I'm ready. I have a great horse in Rett Butler, an 11-year-old, 15-hand bay Arabian gelding. I have a vastly experienced coach, Tammy Robinson, from whom I bought Rett in 2002. At age 62, I've ridden 14 endurance races in California, including two 100-milers—20-Mule Team and Californios—just a few months earlier. So I'm no stranger to mountainous, precipitous terrain; in fact, this is my second attempt at the Tevis, but as adherents of this sport like to say, they wouldn't call it "endurance" if it wasn't tough.

_ Down, Down, Down; Up, Up, Up

By 4:45, our group is mounted and heading out toward the 5:15 a.m. start. Imagine 250 razor-sharp endurance Arabians, in the dark, in the cold, jammed on a narrow track high in the mountains, waiting to be unleashed! I am riding with Tammy (on Charutu), Tammy's husband, Charlie (riding Rett's full sister Lady), and Don Bowen (on Rett's half-brother Wyatt). Somewhere behind us at the start lineup is a legend of the sport, 80-year-old Julie Suhr, making her twenty-fourth Tevis Cup attempt on Rett's younger, full sister Tara.

The beginning of any endurance race is semi-controlled pandemonium, and this one is no different. Tammy's goal for our group is to start out fast enough to avoid getting trapped behind hundreds of riders, jammed in the narrow, dust-choked single track. In the gray half-light of midsummer dawn, dimmed even further by great swirls of thick dust thrown up by hundreds of churning hooves, I pull a bandana over my face. Some riders wear painter's masks, and within minutes of the start of the race, all of us are brown with dirt. Rett can tolerate horses galloping past with equanimity, but ahead of me, Wyatt canters sideways in anxiety. Down and down we go, weaving in and around the narrow trail, barely avoiding trees that threaten to remove riders' kneecaps. After about nine miles, we emerge into the brief respite of Squaw

Valley. Then it's up, up, up through forests of huge pines, skirting the edge of the mountain high above the ski lodges until we emerge under the Squaw Valley ski lift.

Now we climb in earnest, using our horses' heart monitors to modulate the severity of the effort. We adjust our ride to the heart rate of the weaker horses in our little group, because Charutu is a heart rate "monster," always about 20 to 30 beats per minute slower than normal horses. "He must have a huge heart like Secretariat's," speculates Tammy. Usually she won't tell us what Charutu's pulse is, so as not to discourage us.

I see some heedless riding now, riders racing up this grinding mountain as though they're on motorcycles instead of horses. My friend and riding companion from back east, Nancy Roeber-Moyer, calls this type of blind attack "the red haze" that overwhelms the clear thinking of many highly competitive personalities. The second vet check—Robinson Flat at 36 miles—sees the elimination of many of these riders who are too exuberant too early.

Finally, above the ski lift we reach the summit. It's a setting of panoramic splendor, I'm sure, if we could take a moment to savor it. We don't. We're about to plunge into an unforgiving and treacherous stretch of seemingly impossible trail. It's my least-favorite section of the entire Tevis Cup: the Granite Chief Wilderness.

_ 50 More Posts

Have you ever walked along the Maine coast, out onto a granite jetty thrusting into the Atlantic Ocean, clambering over slabs and shards of tilted and twisted rocks? If so, you have some idea of what this stretch of trails entails. I don't let myself look down; if I do, I'll try to direct Rett's path between the rocks, which can only throw him off his own decision-making process. I hang on, look up, stay back and hope he stays on his feet. All around me, I hear clanging, scraping, clashing steel-clad hooves on slippery rock.

Working with Cosy Dell Arabians in Waimumu, New Zealand

By Kendall Szumilas

*As we all know, there are two ways to enter a swimming pool.
One way is first a toe, then a foot, then an ankle....
The other, favored by the wild and wooly, is to go charging off
the end of the diving board, take what comes.
The sky can be the limit for those brave and daring enough to take the flying leap.
When Kendall Szumilas graduated from high school in coastal Maine,
she wanted adventure before college, and she discovered
a sort of working student/apprenticeship chance 9,000 miles away,
which involved training young Arabian endurance horses in New Zealand.*

– Denny Emerson –

After high school I craved adventure. My older sister had learned about a website called WWOOF, which stands for World-Wide Opportunities on Organic Farms. The site acts as a way to connect to farms all over the world. The arrangements are different at each farm, but most offer free housing and food in exchange for work around the farm.

After some consideration, I decided to buy a membership to WWOOF New Zealand. From there, I could look at farm profiles and decide what best fit my interests. After some research, I found Cosy Dell Arabians, owned by Trevor Copland.

I stayed at Trevor's farm for six months, and wish I could have stayed longer. Cosy Dell Arabians is a breeding program specializing in endurance racing. At the time I was there, Trevor ran a farm with about 80 horses. They were born in the fields and started when they were about four years old. These horses were unusual in that they knew nothing of humans until then.

The work wasn't just starting young horses, it was starting young, untouched Arabians. You learn to be highly sensitive, calm, and aware when you work with this breed—when to apply pressure and when to remove it. They're challenging, but the reward is worth it. Trevor had a unique approach to working with horses. He was patient and listened to them, and he trained with an understanding of what they knew as horses. He always said that they are allowed to take as much time as they need to take a step forward, but once they've stepped forward, as a trainer you have to encourage them not to go

New Beginnings

back. Go as slowly in training as you need to; don't rush the process. His method worked well. The horses we backed in the previous set were used to pony the next set. It was a cycle, but every horse took a new approach and a different length of time to train.

I had no idea going to New Zealand would so profoundly shape the way I work with horses. I would never trade my experience at Cosy Dell Arabians for anything. My advice for those of you thinking about getting out there and learning is this: Do it. Don't wait for the perfect opportunity to arise, because it never will. Make things happen and enjoy the life you create for yourself. ◆

— Goethe wrote, "Whatever you can do, or dream you can, begin it. Boldness has genius, power, and magic in it." When Kendall Szumilas graduated from high school in coastal Maine, she craved adventure. Lots of teenagers crave adventure, but few of them put in motion the plans to shore up the dreams. Kendall did. Which is why she was able to be her own version of Alec Ramsey, galloping an Arabian along a beach in faraway New Zealand. ▲

| 8 | Begin to Try the Impossible

161

I know this without a doubt: not one of all my hundreds of friends and acquaintances in three-day eventing would ever consider taking their event horses over this 20-mile stretch of the Tevis Cup trail that I've just negotiated—and we're not even a quarter of the way home. It's only going to get a lot tougher, because as each hard mile upon hard mile looms, we're doing those hard miles on increasingly tired horses. This, I think, is what makes the Tevis Cup so much more arduous than all the other endurance races I've done (some 38 over the past seven years). There's no respite, only one challenge piled upon another.

A lot of endurance riding is just hanging in there. They tell you to ride "chunks" of the ride, from one vet check to the next; it's too mentally overwhelming to think, "I've got 67 miles to go." It's easier to think, "I've only got 13 miles to go to Michigan Bluff." That you can handle; the other is emotional overload. Or you can break it down into even smaller bite-size bits. "I can trot 25 more strides to that broken tree stump—no matter how much my knees are burning—then 50 more posts to the black rock." Then do it again. And again.

What's hurting me at this point in the ride: my feet, my back, and especially my knees from having them braced out in front for all the downhill trotting. There are a million rocks, from little fist-sized ones to rocks bigger than basketballs. There's an endurance saying that "one of them has your name on it." Rett has gone down hard

on his knees and his nose a couple of times in the past, so I know the meaning of that saying. A fall can end my ride in a heartbeat. I don't want Rett to somersault. I try to stay vigilant; I don't want to get out of balance with him, and the physical and mental toll increases with the hours.

There's a toll on the horses, too, which is the reason for mandatory vet holds. The race has nine vet checks (including the finish), but two of these include an actual required rest—a one-hour hold. Each of the nine checks has a criterion, a predetermined number of heart beats per minute that your horse has to achieve before the veterinarians will even look to decide if he can continue. Since your horse's pulse is elevated from work on the trail, this means his pulse has to come down. At the checks that require a rest, your one-hour hold time doesn't even start until you reach the criterion, a moment that's called "pulsing in."

At Robinson Flat, that criterion is 60. To help Rett get "down," Bry Cardello and Tina Fransioli, my crew from back east, sponge his neck and chest with cold water. Then, 60 beats achieved, we go in front of the vets. They listen to Rett's gut sounds, press on his gums for capillary refill, do a skin-tenting pinch test for hydration, watch him trot for soundness, and track a cardio-recovery index to make sure his pulse stays down and is not spiking (a sure sign of distress).

I go sit in the shade while Bry and Tina tempt Rett with an equine smorgasbord so he can refuel for the miles ahead.

_ Canyons: Only Dangerous If You Crash

About halfway through the ride, we finally come to the infamous canyons, which are essentially huge bowls within the mountains carved out millions of years ago by glaciers moving along stream-beds. To this day, the American River runs through these canyons.

There is much lore and legend about the dangers of falling off the edges of the narrow trails that skirt these precipitous canyons, and as we ride switchback after switchback into the bowels of the mountain landscape, I can see why. It is true that there is constant danger, but without downplaying it, I would say that it is the same danger inherent in flying in an airplane: It's only dangerous if you crash. These horses don't want to crash any more than we riders want them to.

Once in a great while, it is true, accidents happen, but very rarely. How else to say it? Yes, riding the canyon is dangerous. No, accidents don't happen very often. I could say the same thing about my 43 seasons of three-day eventing. "Yes, a horse could flip over a fence and land on me. No, it hasn't happened yet." On the really steep places, I simply don't look down. I'm not terrified of heights like some people are, but I'm not in love with them, either!

Clawing out of the two canyons is the most physically gut-wrenching part of the ride. At the summit of each pull is a water hold and a chance to let our horses rest and eat for a few minutes. Pretty soon, we'll come to our second one-hour hold, at Forest Hill, also our last daylight vet check. (We're giving our horses unrequired rests, too, at some of the other vet checks. The winning riders probably haven't.)

_ Making Haste Slowly

Riding in the dark changes the whole equation. It's ever so much slower, and the rock with your name on it becomes invisible, too. Unless I'm lost or it's raining, I love riding at night. This night, the huge full moon is like a searchlight. Far below, we glance downward and catch a glimpse of the silver ribbon of river. We can hear its constant roar, now louder, now fainter, as the trail drops or ascends.

At the Francisco's vet check (mile 86), Rett pulses in at criterion 68, but then his pulse rate fails to keep dropping. It bounces up and down—69, 70, 73, 69—but stays higher than I like. He's also ravenously hungry. I decide to stay, let him eat and wait until his pulse gets consistently into the 50s before going on. I've gotten this far; I don't want to jeopardize our chance of finishing, even with a slower time. (It's a good time to remember the American Endurance Ride Conference motto: "To finish is to win.") Tammy and Don press on. I stay.

After about half an hour, Rett's pulse is down and I head out, worried that he's so bonded to Wyatt and Charutu that he'll whinny and fret without them. Luckily, I fall in with Kelly Blue, whose horse, like Rett, is tired but okay. Kelly tells me that at each of the last two Tevis rides, she's gotten to the last vet check, the Quarry at mile 94, and been pulled. We agree that we're going to ride smart and not suffer that fate. We walk or trot—"make haste slowly" would be our motto. We know the ride cutoff isn't until 5:15 a.m., and we're well within that time frame.

Tevis vets are known to give no quarter, nor should they. It's too unforgiving a race to let compromised horses carry on. Kelly and I are increasingly optimistic but afraid to voice it. There are malignant gods waiting to crush you. *Hubris*. The Greeks called it "pride followed by destruction." This night, we aren't going to summon those lightning strikes!

We pulse in and jog through the vetting at the Quarry. Now we can taste it. Six more miles. We cross No Hands Bridge in the blinding moonlight and begin one more endless climb toward Auburn, the Fairground finish line. "Just around the corner" takes forever.

Suddenly my watch starts to beep. It's my 3:45 alarm from yesterday morning, 98 miles ago. We climb the last ridge, and Kelly yells into the darkness, "Whoohee!" An answering yell from somewhere up above. We're there. Lights. People.

We emerge from the dense blackness of the forest, see the flow of lights from the fairground, and hear people cheering and clapping at our arrival. Even at four in the morning there's a small welcoming crowd. We walk across a road and down the slope to enter the brightly lit oval below the grandstand. Rett comes alive as he trots his lap of honor strongly once around the track, totally sound, ears pricked. I dismount and lead him to the final vet check.

Dr. Ray Randle finishes his examination, puts his stethoscope into his shirt pocket, smiles, and puts out his hand. "Congratulations," he says.

We've done it, the fiftieth anniversary of the Tevis Cup, although it won't really sink in for some days.

As I put little Rett to bed in his stall after all his gallant effort over these past 23 hours, I remember once again Tammy's statement about world-class endurance horses: "It's like riding a miracle." ◆ ◆ ◆

BEGIN

Your Bucket List

Many riders, as they gain stature and experience in some horse sport or breed, get asked to judge or otherwise officiate at various local competitions.

9

__ Give Your Dreams a Chance

Here's a list of some adventures you can have with horses. It's by no means complete, but these are some that I've done:

- Drive cattle
- Ride at night
- Drive a sleigh
- Play polo
- Go foxhunting
- Race on the flat
- Race over jumps
- Swim with your horse
- Ride in the ocean
- Ride in a competitive trail or an endurance ride
- Ride 100 miles in one day
- Ride saddle seat
- Ride bareback
- Breed a mare and raise a foal
- Ride in a dressage show

— My saddle seat riding career was early and brief. It began in 1957 when I was showing Lippitt Sandy in various Morgan classes, continued in 1958, 1959, 1960, and ended in 1961 with Vermont Governor Deane Davis's Lippitt Tweedle Dee being my last foray into that specialized type of riding. One thing that it taught me was the ability to control two reins, snaffle and curb, and to have hands soft as a floating feather. This photo shows a competitor at the Oklahoma City Morgan Grand National. ▼

— These are some of the words that we use to describe the good distance horses: *game, gritty, generous, brave, tough, gutsy.* They are words of praise, as they all should be. Tammy Robinson's summation, "It's like riding a miracle," might sound overblown, but when you are climbing out of some rocky canyon at midnight and you feel your horse dig in and get it done, "miracle" is exactly the right word for a horse like my Tevis Cup partner Rett Butler. ▲

- Drive a sulky
- Drive a pair
- Ride in an event
- Ride in a jumper show
- Gallop a racehorse
- Camp overnight with your horse
- Be a ringmaster
- Try free jumping your horse
- Write a book about horses
- Manage a barn

If you feel stuck in that same old rut, year after year, and you want to break out and try something entirely different, the adventures and missions just listed are some that I have tried. A few of these were short "dabbles," lasting only a few days or weeks, while others became so familiar as to be new learned skills.

There isn't anything sacred about this list. It's just a few of the opportunities that came my way that I decided to try. If you don't find some of these of much interest, find some others. The idea is to have adventures, and you will decide just how far you want to go.

Not every adventure will involve riding or driving or handling an actual horse. Some people will get their horse fix through painting horses, photographing them, writing about them. These are your adventures, and you alone should determine your choices.

_ In 1957, when I was planning to drive Lippitt Sandy in a half-mile race in harness at the National Morgan Horse Show, it occurred to me that I had never driven a horse hitched to a sulky like this one. Francis Kinsman knew a Standardbred trainer with horses at the Franklin County Fairgrounds in Greenfield, Massachusetts. The trainer gave me a driving lesson, and I have two memories from that distant episode: 1) How low to the ground I felt, and 2) how fast a trotter can trot. ▼

With the Horses—and My Camera

By Ashley Neuhof

The hush of the crowd falls over the arena, with only the sound of trotting hoof beats echoing down the tunnel. There is a split-second pass by a solid wall—a clean backdrop with the sun glinting just right as the rider pats the proud and confident animal, striding forth as the announcer calls their names, which brings a deafening roar from thousands of horse sport lovers. Click. These are the moments I live for.

My story begins like many: a horse-crazy girl whose dream it was to ride on the international stage under the Stars and Stripes. And like many, my life took twists and turns away from those dreams, only to eventually land me right back where I was always meant to be: with the horses.

But instead of strapping on my spurs and zipping up my cross-country vest, I fasten lenses into place and triple-check memory cards, batteries, and press passes. With a nod to my assistant photographer, we stride out of the world's most famous horse-sport press room and onto the field at The World Equestrian Festival of the CHIO Aachen. Before we hit the field, I hang back, waiting for that moment of simultaneous calm and tension, just as the gate goes up for the next horse-and-rider pair contesting the gargantuan Grand Prix. These moments bring me back to those tense minutes before a cross-country

round, your heart in your throat, wishing you were any place else but eager to give it your best shot. I know that feeling, and that is what I aim to capture behind the lens. This is my story of finding a life with horses after I hung up my competition boots for the last time.

For more than five years, I have been fortunate enough to travel the world as a professional equestrian sport and lifestyle photographer. The path to this profession manifested through the combination of a film studies major at the University of Vermont and an eventual move to New York City, where I shifted my focus to still photography. One of the most difficult elements in photography is to discover your own niche. In New York, there are thousands of fashion and wedding photographers, all with dynamite portfolios that one can only dream of creating over many years in the field. I had a few friends and mentors encourage me to consider blending my love and knowledge of horses with the photographic medium, and for them I am forever grateful.

One of my first shoots with studio lighting of my own planning was actually done at Denny's farm in Vermont with my friends who worked there at the time. When I achieved some exciting portrait results, I knew I was onto something. I had been searching high and low for work that would stick, with my own interest and creative motivation and with outside viewers.

What took me a while to realize was that it was all staring me straight in the face and, like Dorothy from *The Wizard of Oz*, the passport to a career I could only dream about was right in my backyard.

I began attending some of the show-jumping events in the greater New York area and started building a portfolio, not ever intending to make that the bread and butter of my existence, but it was a very fun weekend activity.

One of the main reasons people are discouraging when it comes to a career as a wedding photographer is that you'll never experience another

—I follow Ashley Neuhof on Facebook. Yesterday, I think, she arrived in Paris. Next week, Pogo Pogo? The point being that having the drive to create a set of skills, and the willingness to hone those skills, has given her an "Open Sesame" to worlds that most horse-addicted kids might only imagine in a dreamscape. ▲

weekend off in your life. This past year, I spent 40 weekends on the road, so that advice did not exactly sink in for me.

One show led to another and I discovered that this was the sport that was waiting for me to make my niche. The jumps were big, the horses exquisitely talented, and the lifestyle lent itself to a compelling story that this little horse-crazy girl from Vermont began to tell.

With my soul anchored but feet aflutter, I dove in and went to Wellington, Florida, one winter, stayed with a family friend, and planted myself in the mecca of horse sport, eager to build up a body of work that would hopefully catch the attention of a few important contacts. I began working for *Horse and Style Magazine* while also shooting my very first cover with Clea Newman for *Untacked*.

My network grew and so did the following of my work. It changed shape and approach multiple times until I arrived at what I would describe as a hybrid of sports lifestyle documentary. Riders and owners began to recognize my work, and a few took the chance to sign up for a personalized documentary-style portfolio of their show season. This would be the beginning of what has become the absolute ride of a lifetime, and I am truly grateful to be able to enjoy horses beyond the competition as a rider myself.

When I work with clients, I become a part of their team. I'm there at the warm-up, snapping frames of those quieter moments as they gather their thoughts and their plan. When the rails stay up, I'm the first one at the tunnel to capture the sheer elation and gratitude they have for their mount and their team. And when it goes wrong, I'm there to remind them why they do this through images that aim to capture their passion for the sport and the animals they love. And when loved ones cannot be there to witness the special moments, it is the greatest honor to be the one to tell the story so they can have a window into that day.

While the trajectory of this profession became quite steep and exciting, I had actually been preparing for this my entire life. It is only recently that I have fully grasped how every element of my childhood, youth, and young adult life have led me to so many "pinch me" moments at some of the biggest competitions in the world, shooting alongside photographers I have admired since I was a little girl.

Many of the riders I have grown up watching in the show-jumping arena on television are luckily still at it, and being able to step onto the field at places like Spruce Meadows and Aachen as they canter into the ring is beyond surreal. Photography is, in its most basic form, the result of someone being in the right place at the right time to capture an instant that is gone forever. For all of us who love and cherish horses, we are always living in moments that are fleeting. Wherever I am in the world, I always pause and think about how I got there and I am forever grateful that horses have led the way. ◆

These are some of the things I haven't done (yet):

- Cutting
- Reining
- Team penning
- Roping
- Saddle bronc
- Bareback bronc
- Five-gaited horse
- Round penning/natural horsemanship
- Mongol Derby
- Roadster pony
- Painted horses
- Sculpted horses
- Braided a tail
- Made a horse video or movie
- Become a pedigree semi-expert about many breeds
- Harnessed a work team
- Plowed
- Sugared
- Mowed hay
- Competed at a horse pull
- Ridden in the Maryland Hunt Cup
- Observed wild horses
- Trained a donkey or a mule
- Ridden in Africa, watching wildlife

Maybe I'll get to them, and maybe I won't. A few of them I know I won't! But they're out there.

⸺ A Montana Backcountry Adventure

Now, if you are an Easterner like me, you probably think of the word "roundup," but when I was visiting Tom and Jesse Alderson in Kirby, Wyoming, Tom asked me if I'd like to go on a "bull gather" at a ranch in Decker, Montana. There were about 600 bulls on about 40,000 acres, and since winter was coming, they needed to be moved from summer range to winter range.

Tom had a Thoroughbred mare named Mimi that he let me use, a great old athlete who'd raced, gone Advanced in three-day eventing, and was good in rough country.

After we trucked two horses down to Decker, we joined a little convoy of rigs to drive several miles up into the mountains so that we'd start the gather close to where the bulls had fanned out over miles of steep, partly wooded terrain.

We split up into smaller groups and headed off in different directions. The guy running the gather pointed to a sharp peak in the distance. "Just head them toward that ridge," he said. "We'll take them in from there."

Horses raised and ridden in that county are shifty and sure-footed, and they'd better be. We picked up a small group of bulls, five or six, and headed them along, picking up more as we went. Some came along, but some broke off to go back into the steep hollows where they'd been, close to water. It was our job to get ahead of them and cut them off. I was cantering Mimi along the edge of what looked like a shale slide when Tim ran by me flat out.

"I'd appreciate a little help, Mr. Emerson."

That was one wakeup call as to what was expected. Another: I was headed down a narrow trail, alone, and it got narrower, with sharp stubs of broken branches hemming us in. I had my head down near Mimi's neck so I wouldn't get stabbed in the face, and suddenly Mimi stopped dead.

I carefully looked up and saw that the trail had ended in about a 6- or 7-foot vertical drop-off, where a flash flood must have come through. There was no room to turn around. There was no way to back up. The only option was to get Mimi to jump off the ledge from a standstill and see what happened.

So, I kicked her, clucked at her, and she teetered back and forth, then leapt off, straight down, landed hard, lunged, and was fine. I'd managed not to get speared by the saddle horn in the process, but I was getting the picture of what you got in backcountry Montana.

But that wasn't the worst.

A little later we were traversing a narrow trail cut into a mountain side. To my left was a wall of rock, almost close enough to rub my left knee. To my right was a steep slide of broken chunks of rock, twisted and gnarled stumps and roots, and loose trap rock.

We came to a section of the trail where a slide had basically torn the trail off the mountain. For 6 or 8 feet, the trail was so narrow that maybe an agile cat could have danced across before it widened. I could see Tom and two others on a plateau ahead, so I yelled at him, "Hey, Tom! How do I get over where you are?"

I was thinking he'd say, "Turn around, go back a mile, turn left," or something along those lines.

Tom yelled back, "Let go of her head and kick her."

Now, there are some things worse than death. One of them is to be from the East and to be revealed as a cowardly chicken in front of Western cowboys.

I let go of her head and kicked her. Mimi lunged and scrambled, caught the wider trail with her front legs, and hauled herself to safety.

Later, I asked Tom, "Don't they sometimes fall when you do that?"

"Oh, yeah."

"What do they do when they fall?"

"They somersault to the bottom."

"What do you do when that happens?"

"Step off on the uphill side."

I figured out how Tom had gone from Beginner Novice to Advanced eventing in two years. The things that he did on a daily basis were riskier than most cross-country courses could ever be.

Later, as we were pushing the bellowing, slow-moving bulls in an endless line back toward the ranch, I asked this one grumpy, grizzled old guy, "What do you feed these bulls during the winter?"

I figured that they would bring out loads of hay after blizzards, or some such.

He spat out a wad of chewing tobacco. "We feed 'em snow and scenery."

You might not want to start your Western adventure on a bull gather in Decker, Wyoming. Build up to it.

Riding at Midnight

In July of 1958, about a month before my seventeenth birthday, I was staying at my parents' remote farm in South Reading, Vermont. Mom and Dad ran Stoneleigh Prospect Hill School in Greenfield, Massachusetts, and they were there during the week, coming to Vermont on weekends, so I often had the place to myself.

One evening, I rode my little Morgan stallion, Lippitt Raymond, down Pucker Street, across the Tyson Road, and out onto Brown Schoolhouse Road, the least built-up part of an already sparsely populated town, especially 60 years ago. It stays light forever that far north in July. I'd lost track of time, exploring some side trails, when I realized

that I was a long way from home, and it was getting dark.

I turned Ray around, but before long it got seriously black out—no moon, filtered starlight, no brightly lit farmhouses to light the way.

I'd read all about what to do if you were lost: just loosen the reins and give your horse his head and let him figure it out. I wasn't particularly nervous. It was a warm July night, not some raging blizzard, and there weren't any wolves or mountain lions, so I figured that sooner or later I'd come out somewhere.

Riding in the dark at a walk in summer woods is strangely peaceful. All you hear is the soft thud of hooves, creaking of leather, light breathing, wind in the pines, calling of the frogs, maybe some crickets.

We walked and walked, and at one point I heard Raymond's hooves clopping on pavement, so I assumed we were crossing Tyson Road on the way home. A little later, I heard the thudding sound of his hooves on wooden planks, and I was pretty sure that we were back on Pucker Street. I could tell that we were climbing even though it was so dark that I couldn't see my hand in front of my face.

Raymond stopped. I gave him a little kick, and he took a step and stopped. I got off and put my hand out in front of me, and touched the granite hitching post in our yard in front of the barn.

They are right about horses knowing how to get home.

_ Melissa Chapman took "back country" riding to a level few will ever know by riding across the entire United States from New York to California (read all about it in her book *Distant Skies*). I watch these videos of perilous adventures like sailing solo across the Pacific, or climbing with no ropes up some rock needle, and I lump what Melissa did right up there with them—so far beyond what most of us can even dream of doing. ▲

There are many degrees of what it means to ride out "in the back of beyond." To an 1840s fur trapper, scrambling down a shale slide in a desolate wilderness, my backcountry version becomes like sitting at a Paris sidewalk cafe. But to riders who never leave the confines of an arena, my version—the hills and valleys of central Vermont, with not a horse or road or electric line in sight—might seem daunting enough.

True wilderness riding requires thousands of acres of true wilderness, and in the United States, that probably eliminates much of the country. But there are still plenty of pockets of semi-wilderness where it's possible to ride for hours in total isolation much of the time, or little-traveled back roads, old logging trails, maybe crossing a paved road now and again, but alone enough and remote enough so that if you got hurt in a fall where there's no cell service, you could be in real trouble.

It's smarter to ride with another person, but that's not always possible, and for some, it negates the idea of solitary wilderness. But you don't want to die of hypothermia or some injury, either, I don't imagine, so there are lots of precautions that you should take if you ride out alone.

Take a cell phone. Not all places get service, and you can't use one if you are unconscious, but better to have one than not. Many riders have two emergency packs, a saddle or pommel bag attached to the horse, the other some sort of fanny pack attached to their own body, in case the horse takes off. Google "endurance riding tack and equipment" to get ideas. Your phone will be hitched to you; that's pretty obvious. Other items that I personally carry include a lighter that works, a small knife or multi-tool, a whistle, and small compass, some nylon twine, a pencil stub, and a small pad of paper. Take water, a small thermal blanket, a bigger multi-tool, some strong but light nylon cord, a mini first aid kit— anything that you think you might need if you get lost or your horse gets hurt or goes lame, and you might need to hole up and wait for help.

I take one of those hoof boots that you can use when your horse loses a shoe. There are bags that hang on the saddle that are made to carry these. Maybe roll up a poncho or raincoat, and tie that on as well. If you are just headed out on a local trail ride for an hour or hour and a half, in a country that is crisscrossed with roads and has houses or farms here and there, it may be overkill to take so much gear. But when the area where you ride is at all remote, and you are going to be out there by yourself, better to be safe than sorry.

How do you find places to ride? This will range all over the lot, from having instant access to state or federal land, to trailing to some trailhead, to living in an already remote area, to belonging to some association, like the Green Mountain Horse Association in South Woodstock, Vermont, which has access to trails and back roads, to having a friend who lives in a less populated area.

In both Southern Pines, North Carolina, and in Strafford, Vermont, I ride on some property that is privately owned and that requires an entire set of behaviors aimed at doing everything possible to continue to be allowed to ride there. There is a saying that nothing is more fragile than a trail network, because all it takes is one locked gate on one landowner's property to spoil it for everyone.

You may have seen the film series *Unbranded*, about four young men who rode Mustangs from the border with Mexico all the way north to the Canadian border. At one point they came to a locked gate. The path through the blocked-off property was only a mile or so, but they had to detour many miles over hard terrain to go around and resume the trail.

Respect the property that you ride across. Never, ever leave any trash. Don't ride across wet fields and leave deep hoof prints. Don't ride through a hay field. Never open a gate and fail to shut it. Always be pleasant to anyone you meet. That person may own the land you're riding on.

There was a recent case of a few girls who were riding on some timberland, and a pickup drove up the road behind them. The truck spooked one of the horses, and the rider screamed at the driver and flipped him off. The driver was the owner of that land and several hundred more acres. Within a week, all access gates were chained and padlocked.

Don't be that person who wrecks it for everyone else.

This same ethic also applies to places where you park your trailer, whether it's a state park, a game preserve, or wherever. Hay dropped from hay nets, manure, trash—pick it up and pack it out. If you can arrive with it, you can leave with it.

Riders and hikers and mountain bikers and users of ATVs, snow machines—they are all competing for access to land, and there is a truism that there are a lot more people who hike and bike than ride horses. So, share, be respectful, and do your part in preserving horse access to open land.

_ Polo

If the word "polo" conjures visions of thundering Thoroughbreds ridden by impossibly glorious young Argentines across sweeping green meadows while elegant spectators sip champagne in front of a line of chauffeur drivers, you never watched my polo team.

Bob Lamb ran Rolling Ridge, a girls' summer riding camp just outside the village of Woodstock, Vermont, back in the mid-1960s. I had a summer riding job at the Mac Williamson's Thoroughbred breeding farm next door, and when Bob was seeking recruits for a polo squad, I was first in line.

Nothing we had matched regulation—not the dimensions of our polo field, not our mallets, not the size or make of the polo balls, not the horses, and most

_ If I were to tap a magic wand to give the aspiring polo player two physical gifts that I found I needed, one would be wrist strength—my right arm would start to ache—and the other would be the ability that horses have to see what's beside and even behind them, because whatever you are trying to do, here comes some opponent trying to prevent you from getting it done. Here's our Rolling Ridge team at Sugarbush in Warren, Vermont, in 1965. ▼

certainly, with one exception, not the skills of the riders.

Our horses were picked from the camp horse string. Just to give you an example, one of the horses was used to pack picnic lunches when the kids were taken on long trail rides. The name of the pack horse, also a part-time polo pony, was U-Haul.

Somehow, I can't see some six-goal player from Long Island screaming down the field on U-Haul.

Anyway, we practiced a couple of evenings each week, using a smaller version of a soccer ball. Our field was just by the Ottauquechee River, and we didn't want the ball to go flying off downstream to wind up in the Atlantic Ocean. The ball had to be "dead" so it didn't go very far when struck hard, not that many of us had the accuracy to do that.

There was only one other polo team in Vermont to compete against: the Sugarbush team in Warren. They had real uniforms, and their field was of regulation size, set decoratively in front of a large Swiss chalet. There was a small pond at one end of the field, which was a good thing for me one particular evening when the part draft horse, faded palomino I was riding took off with me, and the only way I got him stopped was by riding him into the pond.

A Rolling Ridge counselor from Venezuela was our only experienced player. The mission for the rest of us was to try to whack the ball somewhere in that rider's general vicinity so that he could score our only goals.

Despite the rough-and-ready aspects of our general ineptitude, we had enough enthusiasm to counteract lack of skill, and if I had the chance, I would do it again.

_ Driving a Pair

I drove a pair of ponies before I ever drove a single. When we moved to Massachusetts in 1950, from New Hampshire, there was a big red shed on the lane up to Stoneleigh Prospect Hill School, and within the shed was an old four-wheeled horse-drawn vehicle that my father called a "Democrat." The front two wheels were on a swivel, so that they turned independently from the rear wheels. There was enough room in front for two, and enough room for two or three in the back seat.

Three local boys, Paul Barrett, Jack Baker, and I, had all bought ponies from Louis Goodyear down in nearby Sunderland, and for whatever reason, we decided to teach Scout and Chief how to drive as a pair.

Now, remember, we were about 10 or 11. We knew nothing, as in zero, about anything pertaining to driving ponies. I don't even remember where we got the harness, or how we learned to put it on the pair, or what adult helped us. It might have been my father, or the Stoneleigh farm manager, Francis Kinsman, but I think maybe we just hitched them up, got in, and drove away.

It's a darn lucky thing, looking back, that Louis Goodyear was a highly responsible horse dealer. He had a saying, "kid-broke horse," which meant gentle and pretty tolerant, and he wouldn't sell a youngster a pony that Louis didn't think would tolerate mistakes.

In those pre-Interstate 91 days, the Stoneleigh campus had well over 100 acres of land, with a huge hay meadow, trails through the woods, and access to more riding land to the north of the school. Once we got used to driving our little team, we wanted to have outlaws attack the stagecoach. Why wouldn't we? We were young boys. We had an old Army ammunition box, and we painted some rocks with gold spray paint to make a gold-filled strongbox. One kid would drive the stagecoach, another kid had a real (but unloaded) 12-gauge shotgun, and a few more of us would tie bandanas across our faces and chase the stage.

One fateful day, when Jack Baker and I were outlaws, we spooked the team pulling the wagon into a runaway. The trail split right and left, with a few trees in the middle. Paul steered left, the ponies ran right, and the whole rig ran into the trees.

Harness shredded, the cart capsized, little kids, guns, strongbox, gold scattered, the ponies ran off, unhurt. Jack and I saw the wreck, spun our ponies, and with no thought about whether the other kids were alive (they were), we galloped away so that we could have an excuse when it came time to lie to our parents.

Now, as I said, we were 11-, 12-year-old human males, nothing dumber than which

⎯ It's easy to grasp why the horseless carriage became such a hit. You get in, shut the door, turn the key, and off you go. Not so for a pair. First you have to fetch each pony. Then you groom them. Then you get the many bits and pieces of harness and try to figure out how and where to strap and attach them. Then you have to get the cart. Then you have to get the ponies to stand still while you attach them to the cart. Now, finally, you are ready to climb in. But here's the good news: You don't need to turn the key, so there's that time- and labor-saving advantage! Chief and Scout were the first ponies I ever drove as a pair. ▲

exists. So, don't turn your pair-driving venture into a runaway stagecoach. And maybe learn how to drive a pair from someone who knows how.

Or you can try it our way and see what happens.

_ Ride on the Beach and in the Ocean

The only time that I've ever done this was at Crane's Beach, in Ipswich, Massachusetts, way back in 1975 or 1976, when I was training at the old USET Three-Day Team headquarters in South Hamilton.

Jack Le Goff believed in the therapeutic benefits of cold salt water, and once in a while, he'd have the farm manager Patrick Lynch drive the big USET van over to the beach at the times of the year when horses were allowed.

I've seen lots of photos of horses galloping on beaches, down where the sand is hard at the tide line, but Jack was a little too cautious to have us do that, because of all the flotsam that beaches collect—worst of all, glass bottles and planks with nails. So first, we walked and trotted about a mile or so to check the general footing, after which we'd turn and canter back in sets of two or three.

The thing that spooked Victor Dakin was being attacked by breaking waves. As each wave crashed, and the line of water would roll onto the beach, Victor would shy, spin, or back pedal to escape. He wasn't afraid of the water, I think. It was the movement that he didn't like. Once I got him to follow Mary Anne Tauskey's tough little horse Marcus Aurelius and got him to actually go into the ocean, he settled down and splashed along quite happily.

Years earlier, I'd been in a boat off the Connecticut shore and seen the kids actually swimming their horses in the surf. They'd gallop down the beach into the water, riding bareback in bathing suits, timing it just right to run head on into cresting and crashing waves. It was obvious that the horses were used to doing it, because they had no fear or hesitation.

And who hasn't watched those scenes from *The Black Stallion* movie, after the shipwreck, when the Black swims to the island, towing little Alec Ramsey to safety?

So, if you live near an ocean, go ride in it. I still haven't swum a horse in an ocean, but at least I had the chance to wade in light surf, and to gallop along a shoreline.

_ Riding Bareback

Long before there were saddles, humans rode horses, so riding bareback is hardly something new or unusual. That said, I think that it's much easier on younger, fitter bodies than older, less flexible ones, so if you are not some wiry teenager, try it for sure, but be careful! The other day, I was watching my granddaughter Abby, trotting around bareback on the little Morgan mare Roxie, and it brought back memories of my first pony

_ Riding bareback is the purest form of riding there is. It is your body and the body of the horse, and there's nothing but 1/80th of an inch of cloth keeping you apart. You want to body-meld with the living, breathing horse? You wish to be the human part of a centaur? Ditch the saddle. Abby, here, and I both were lucky enough to learn this when we were 11 years old. ▼

Paint and how easy it had seemed for the 11-year-old me in 1952, compared to how I think it would feel now, 68 years later. It's not just that little kids have flexible bodies. Little kids don't over-think their riding. They aren't paralyzed by the need to do everything right, so they just ride. They learn to feel and balance on a trotting pony not by trying, but by doing.

There's an old saying that a horse is a horizontal shock-wave producing machine, and the human rider is a vertical shock-wave absorbing machine. As the pony moves, the rider moves, and pretty soon the rider and the pony move in sync with each other, the two bodies melding into one. The less the rider thinks about this, the more the rider just lets it happen, the smoother and faster the process. So, yes, ride bareback, but ride a steady horse if you have any doubts, and see where it goes.

_ Drive a Sleigh

Requirement Number 1: snow. There isn't much sleigh travel in the tropics. But if you live where there's a real winter, and you live where there are dirt roads with minimal car traffic, your next requirement is to have a sleigh and a horse trained to pull it. Then, add sleigh bells, warm robes, maybe some hot cider, and off you go.

My father was born in Danvers, Massachusetts, in 1905, and when he was a boy, he remembered horse-drawn pungs, work sleighs, being pulled by teams of horses, hauling produce on what is now Route 1 from North Shore towns into Boston.

So it was an easy decision for Dad to buy the little sleigh that a retired banker had for sale in Greenfield, Massachusetts, in 1958. The seller told Dad, "Now, Ed, this is a courting sleigh that my grandfather had built in 1830. Do you know the definition of a courting sleigh? Big enough for one, strong enough for two."

South Reading, Vermont, provided lightly traveled dirt roads, and the Morgan gelding Millers Commander (Bongo) was there to pull the sleigh.

I found driving the sleigh a little trickier than driving a wheeled cart on dirt, mainly because the footing is slippery and the sleigh skids out on the turns. Plus, packed snowballs break out of the horse's hind hooves and come flying back at you. And you need to dress warmly—your hands and face get cold when it's 10 degrees and windy.

But for the true Currier and Ives experience, there's nothing better than a brisk trot, the snow squeaking, bells a-jingle, through white New England woods.

Robert Frost, of course, said it best in "Stopping by Woods on a Snowy Evening":

Whose woods these are I think I know.
His house is in the village though;
He will not see me stopping here
To watch his woods fill up with snow.

My little horse must think it queer
To stop without a farmhouse near
Between the woods and frozen lake
The darkest evening of the year.

He gives his harness bells a shake
To ask if there is some mistake.
The only other sound's the sweep
Of easy wind and downy flake.

The woods are lovely, dark and deep,
But I have promises to keep,
And miles to go before I sleep,
And miles to go before I sleep.

_ Join a Local Horse Club, Discipline Association, or Breed Organization

"Birds of a feather stick together." We've all heard that one, and it's relevant in the smorgasbord of the horse world, where there are so many different breeds, and users, and disciplines, and sports. The two big ones are discipline organizations, like the USEA (US Eventing Association) for eventing, the USDF (US Dressage Federation) for dressage, and breed associations like the AQHA (American Quarter Horse Association) for Quarter Horses, or the AMHA (American Morgan Horse Association) for Morgans. When I say, "big ones," I am not counting the international or national federations like the FEI (*Fédération Équestre Internationale*) or the USEF (United States Equestrian Foundation), because these are not so relevant to many riders, drivers, or horse owners. Sure, they are there, and yes, some get involved, but for general observation I am sticking with groups or clubs that seem more within the grasp of average riders.

It's quite normal to be a member of, say, the AMHA, if you have a Morgan, and also the USDF, if you do dressage with your Morgan, and also some local club like the Champlain Valley Dressage Association, which hosts local shows in Vermont.

Some people ride in solitude, never compete, and have little need of horse clubs, while others are joiners and activists and not only belong to various horse associations, but are also active within them as volunteers, board members, or club officials.

You can get as involved as you want. The most common first step is to volunteer at a show or clinic being hosted by your club, and don't be surprised if you get to spend the day in some muddy parking lot trying to get competitors who can't back their trailer without jack-knifing to park *here* rather than *there*.

The thankless types of jobs can be thought of as paying your dues. The funny thing is that very often it will be the club president out slopping around doing the least glamorous jobs—part of the reason that he is the club president. There's a standing joke that the president of the club that's running the show is the guy standing out in the field parking horse trailers. This leaves the more fun stuff for the volunteers.

If you keep showing up, it's almost inevitable that you will get promoted to first assistant jump-rail painter, then to timer or scorer, and so on, until you either run far away or get elected to the governing body.

All these clubs, organizations, associations desperately need volunteer labor, so if you were looking to get more involved, join something and ask what you can do to help.

_ Volunteering

There are a number of ways to volunteer with horses: at a horse show, long-distance ride, event, rodeo, or other sorts of competition. Like clubs and organizations, most competitions ride on the backs of their volunteers. If they had to pay everyone who helps, they couldn't afford to run them.

Here are a few jobs. Some require a strong back, others a sharp mind. Pick the one that seems interesting.

- Dressage judges need scribes. The judge will give a score and make a short comment, and you write it down.

- Veterinarians at trail rides or events also need scribes. Scribing is a good way to get educated while you are filling a need.

- Lots of competitions need timers: three-day events, trail rides, barrel races, show jumping. Have stopwatch, will travel.

- Jumping competitions need a jump crew. You load jumps onto flatbed trailers, take them into the arena, set them up where directed, and remove them after the class is done.

- Or be part of a construction crew, building cross-country jumps for the sport of eventing. Can you drive a tractor, operate a bucket loader? There's a need for you. Good with a hammer and shovel? Your skills are also in demand.

- Perhaps you are good with adding machines? You can become a scorer at various competitions.

- Like to interact with people? Help in the secretary's booth, take entries, hand out numbers and competition packets.

- Many local clubs have a promotion booth that sells T-shirts, books, hats, coffee mugs. These places often need help.

The point is that from painting jumps to parking cars, from using brains to using brawn, there is always,

Starting Over: Stories from Re-Riders

NICKU BRUCE

I've navigated the road from baby to back in the saddle twice in the recent years. Succeeding at riding and motherhood is such a challenge, and moms feel a lot of "Mom Guilt." For every choice we make, there is someone cheering us on and someone else giving us serious side-eye. I'm in a couple of mom rider groups on Facebook, and we all agree that it's difficult when the kids are little.

Go for your goals, Mama! I've had four pregnancies in five years, resulting in two boys. Riding after babies takes grace and grit and a group of people to help you out. After my second son was born—about 12 weeks post C-section—I got a great trainer, half-leased a schoolmaster, and earned my USDF Bronze Medal. Accept the help of your partner, friends, and trainer, make the most of whatever time you get in the saddle, get fit outside the barn, stay grateful and focused. It can be done! ◆

Starting Over: Stories from Re-Riders

SHELLY TEMPLE

I missed riding. Previously, I had driven and competed seriously at the FEI level in Combined Driving since 1997. I rode out for a hack once a month or so, but I hadn't ridden or shown in dressage for over 15 years. As much as I loved driving, I missed being close to my horse, being able to give him a pat or feel him underneath me.

I was asked to scribe for USEF dressage judge Amy McElroy at a driving show. Dressage is dressage, ridden or driven. Amy offered to help me on the journey back to ridden dressage with my Morgan pony Cooper. Amy loved Cooper right away, but I'm sure she saw that her work was cut out for her in helping me. I had not ridden for so long that I was badly out of shape. I lacked flexibility and had gained 20-plus pounds since my riding days. My sitting trot, which had never been a problem in my younger days, was horrible; I was stiff and bouncing.

It's one thing to be a beginner not knowing how bad you are as you slowly work toward getting better. It's another, very humbling experience to know what your body needs to do, realize the requests you are making of your body are being totally ignored, and truly realize just how badly you are riding. "Embrace the Suck" became my daily mantra. I felt sorry for Cooper, but he was so forgiving. I slowly became fitter and more flexible and lost weight. My sitting trot improved. I knew that I wouldn't ever be as flexible as I was in my youth, but I kept working on it day by day.

During that time, of course, life got in the way, with time and health issues and Cooper having surgery to remove an abdominal lipoma. Still we moved forward. Together Cooper and I got our Bronze and Silver Medals and competed up to Intermediate I. At 63, it's still work to stay fit and strong. Cooper has stepped down to trail riding at 22, and I have a young horse, Shady, to continue to ride as long as I can. Shady doesn't drive yet. Always an option in the future. For now I will enjoy every day I spend riding. ◆

always a need for a willing volunteer. It's a good way to get involved, to meet new fellow horse people, and to learn more about a sport, a breed, or a style of riding. But you have to be careful. If you do too good a job, you will get elected club president, and you'll find yourself in some muddy field parking cars.

— Becoming a Judge, a Steward, or Some Other Official

Many riders, as they gain stature and experience in some horse sport or breed, get asked to judge or otherwise officiate at various local competitions. If this has been your situation and you feel that you have both interest and aptitude, you may want to take this to a higher level.

Most of the "Big Organizations," the ones that administer a breed or a sport, will have specific training programs, seminars, clinics, apprentice judging opportunities, with tests leading to various levels of accreditation. I have had former students who have gone through years of incremental and rigorous practice, passing hard tests at various levels, who have become judges at the world's most prestigious three-day events, including Badminton and the Olympic Games. The sky is the limit for those with drive, ambition, and the willingness to strive to acquire an educated eye.

Becoming a judge confers a great obligation, because judges can literally change the entire direction of a breed of horses, depending upon which horses they pin. There are stories of breeds that have blindly followed new trends, and have suffered, and there are other judges who have held breeds or disciplines to a high standard.

Before deciding to become a judge, think through this quote from Winston Churchill about teachers—it applies equally to judges: "Teachers have powers at their disposal with which prime ministers have not been invested."

There's nothing about this to enter into lightly.

Ride in a Different Saddle

Generally, dressage riders do not herd cows. Saddle seat riders do not gallop Thoroughbreds. Event riders do not drive pack horses. Distance riders do not ride show jumpers.

So by saying "ride in a different saddle," I mean that literally and figuratively, and this may be a hard stretch for all those stuck in a rut who don't want to be trapped there, but who are afraid to make the break. There's safety and comfort in the boring, old familiar.

But what might be fun to try? Never mind right now the logistical difficulties. Those can wait. What might you want to try if there were no major obstacles? Make a list of three or four, because, why not?

The idea is to start by defining some possibilities. We can deal with the logistics later, because the main point of this is to be open to learning a type of riding that may be totally unfamiliar, and then, by extension, somewhat daunting.

What are some different saddles, the actual types that are used for different purposes? In "Western" saddles, there are roping saddles, basic ranch work saddles, reining, cutting, and perhaps other types. "English" saddles are similarly specialized by the type of riding: dressage, jumping, "all purpose," saddle seat, endurance, and other types.

Each saddle, depending how it is crafted, will put the rider in a different position on the horse. Try to use the saddle designed for the type of riding you are doing.

Breed a Mare, Raise a Foal

The people who breed mares and then raise the resulting foals are the bedrock foundation of the entire world of horses, setting aside the fact that wild horses seem pretty capable of getting it done without ever seeing a human being.

But for practical purposes, the horse breeder who is an analytical thinker and who enters into the venture with education

Field Notes

About That Lower Leg

— At 81, in 2021, Mike Plumb continues to ride, train, and teach. He, Bernie Traurig, and a few others world-wide have influenced successive generations of riders. I've been lucky enough to have learned from both Mike and Bernie. ▼

I recently was asked about lower-leg security, and here goes an attempt to explain it.

When I started jumping back in 1961, 60 years ago, my stirrups were too long, I had too much knee contact, and every picture showed my lower legs sliding back toward the horse's hips.

Anyway, by watching better riders, very specifically eight-time Olympian Mike Plumb, I noticed how that area of his leg down by the Achilles tendon stayed in contact with the actual body of the horse just behind the girth, and it remained there, like a solid base, throughout the phases of the jump.

So I messed around with stirrup length until I could feel that contact. What surprised me was how light and loose my knee had to be to

Denny Emerson | *Begin and Begin Again*

achieve the feeling. You can have the knee on, or lower leg on, but you can't have both parts on at the same time.

When I practiced this new way, I concentrated just on that one thing, keeping that knobby ankle-bone, Achilles-tendon part of my leg smack-dab THERE, no movement allowed. I found that made other parts of my body sort of rotate around that key contact point, but having that base gave me a sense of security that I had never before experienced. ◆

and insight is the mainstay of both the breeds and the disciplines. But only if you do it right.

Every year, all over the world, thousands of horses wind up in what are sometimes called "kill pens." These are the horses that nobody wants to ride or drive or use for breeding. They have reached the end of the line and will be slaughtered for meat. Nobody likes to talk about this—and neither do I—but that doesn't make it less of a reality.

Now, many of the horses are too old or too sick or too injured to use, but plenty of them are young and sound and simply unwanted. They are horses that have been figuratively "thrown away" by their owners, and the last thing any breeder should do is to breed a foal that has a fair chance of becoming a reject. What turns a horse into a reject? That, it seems to me, is the very first question any breeder should ask before making the decision to breed a specific mare to a specific stallion.

Lack of soundness is number one. Or two, after sanity, but let's call it number one because you can't do anything with an unsound horse except feed it. If the mare was a sound athlete with straight legs and strong hooves, and the sire was a good athlete with straight legs and tough hooves, and both of them stayed sound while in actual use, you are probably okay. If one of the two was basically sound but had a legitimate injury, that's different than when the mare or stallion was chronically unsound because of some structural deficiency.

It becomes important to understand structural conformation, straight legs, and balance—what we might call physical integrity. If you don't know this, be guided by someone who does. Don't breed some crooked-legged mare to some crooked-legged stallion just because they are both some pretty color or

A Whim That Became a Career

BY LESLIE ELLIS

*My early encounters with English saddles, starting about 1957,
were more a necessity than a pleasure. Think hard as a cinder block
and slippery as a block of ice, and you wouldn't be far off the mark.
For decades, I tried so many different saddles, and some were more
comfortable but put my legs too far forward or back; others were
better balanced, but hard and less adapted to hours of riding.
About 20 years ago, I discovered Stackhouse saddles, the small company
that Leslie Ellis is so closely involved with, and for the first time,
all the stars seemed to align. Not to say that there aren't other wonderful
modern saddles, but Leslie makes some that work for me.
She's an example of someone in the horse industry
who doesn't spend her days riding, but she spends plenty
of time in the company of horses and their owners,
and helps make good riding possible for others.*

– DENNY EMERSON –

I did not set out with the intention to become a saddle maker.

I grew up riding but never really considered a horse-related career. I was on an academic path to a regular job as a lawyer, a physical therapist—I'm not really sure what. My goal seemed to change from day to day.

Along the way, I got the notion to take a saddlery course, thinking that it would be fun, and nice to be able to repair my own tack and maybe make some little things. Not far into the course I discovered that I loved working with leather and

had some aptitude for it—I'm detail-oriented, patient, and enjoy the creative process.

My path took another fortuitous turn when I met David Stackhouse and my real training began. David taught me the way he had been taught when he began his traditional six-year apprenticeship in 1962 at the age of 15. However, my apprenticeship was even more valuable because I was taught the "why" along with the "how."

We make completely custom saddles, which means we personally fit each horse and rider.

As a result, I have the satisfaction of creating something, with the added benefit of spending time with some fabulous horses and horse people, often in some of the most beautiful parts of the country. I could not have imagined that acting on a whim would lead to such an interesting and fulfilling career. ◆

— Leslie Ellis writes, "I did not set out with the intention of being a saddle maker." That resonates with me. I think few of us are like the little kid who knows at age 12 that she wants to be a nuclear physicist and 20 years later, she is one. Most of us weave and amble, make false starts, rewind, and, if we are lucky, we find a path that brings daily joy. There are lots of ways to spend time around horses that bring joy, if we can just find the way. ▲

because someone told you that they had "good breeding." Do you want that foal to wind up in some dark place? Of course, you don't, so start with a thorough soundness evaluation.

Now let's go back to sanity, or temperament, or tractability—the qualities of mind and manners that will determine if the young horse will be easy to train. Temperament can be "tricky" to ascertain, because a poor human trainer, or a series of them, can turn the nicest horse into a neurotic mess. If the prospective mother was a nice mare to ride or drive and if she had an actual job to do, she did her work in a positive manner, and, as we've already talked about, she stayed sound doing that job, you are probably okay. But if the mare was hot, balky, hard to ride, if she reared, bucked, rushed at jumps or quit time after time, do you really want to breed those features down the line?

And then there is general athleticism. You may remember that horrible experience from grade school, where there were two captains and a bunch of kids. The captain of the red team would pick a kid. Then the blue team captain would choose, and so on, until there would be two or three "last choice" kids who just were not athletic.

You want to breed a prospective athlete, whether for reining or dressage or whatever. Don't breed the non-athlete to another non-athlete and expect an athletic foal.

And then there is "breed type," if you are staying within a specific breed. The little Arabian should look like an Arabian, the Connemara like a Connemara, and so forth. You will need to understand the standards of your particular breed, and this will be in addition to soundness, sanity, and athleticism.

Wow! Lots to know. And there's more....

Some breeds, or lines within breeds, have underlying genetic time bombs, tendencies toward swaybacks, disease, weak tendons, even sudden death.

But let's say that you have chosen a good mare, and you have scoured the internet, gone to shows, picked the brains of people you trust, and decided on a stallion that seems to complement your mare in all ways—looks, talent, ability, has a compatible rather than a too-inbred pedigree, and so on. Can you afford the stud fee? If not, keep looking. Next, is he available live cover, shipped, cooled semen, or frozen semen? Do you know the percentage of those three in terms of expected live foals after eleven months? Twenty percent? Fifty percent? Seventy-five percent? Do you know what costs are associated with the three "delivery systems"? It's so easy to think that you breed the mare, she gets in foal, and less than a year later, bingo, a perfect little baby appears in your barn, and sometimes that's exactly how it goes. But sometimes, the mare does not get in foal the first time she's bred. Or the second, or the third. Sometimes never. And the vet bills keep growing and growing. You could have gone out and bought a living horse for the money you've spent trying to get your mare to catch.

Or, worse, she does get in foal and aborts. Or has a foal with some deformity. I promise you, I am not being needlessly negative, but I want you to go into this venture, if you do, eyes wide open. This isn't Walt Disney World here. When it works, it can be wonderful. When it doesn't, it can be miserable. It probably works more than it fails, but there is an old, old truism: "Breeding is not for the faint of heart." I would add another: Breeding isn't—or shouldn't be—done on an uneducated whim.

Look, there are hundreds of thousands of wonderful horses in the world, and all of them are the results of breeding, so it absolutely can work. Just be smart and realistic, that's all we ask.

... Owning, Leasing, Half-Leasing, or Borrowing by the Ride

There are all sorts of ways to get access to horses. Some are simple and inexpensive compared to full horse ownerships.

Buying and owning your own horse, if you can afford it, is the way to have the full horse experience. All this, however, comes at a cost, and not just one cost, but plenty of them. First, there's the purchase price, anywhere from free to literally several million dollars. Then the cost of keeping the horse, which can be in a shed behind your house, to a low-, medium-, or high-end boarding stable, to owning your own farm. Then shoeing, veterinary care, tack, equipment, transport, showing costs—it's almost open-ended how much it can cost to own one horse for one year.

If you are on a rock-bottom minimum budget and do all your own care, and have minimum veterinary and farrier care provided, have a turnout shed instead of a barn, you just might be able to scrimp by for less than $10 a day, which comes to something around $3,500 a year.

If you amortize a half-million-dollar horse, board him at a big name show stable, show extensively, and have air fare to Europe, there's almost no limit to what you might spend, but it will easily exceed $100,000 dollars a year. ◆ ◆ ◆

BEGIN

to Embrace What Still Could Be

Everything I had been doing was based on too much—too much force, too much pressure, too much too soon, too much assumption that my horse knew what I wanted but was simply not doing it right, too much, too much. I wasn't teaching, I was forcing.

10

_ Along the Way, a Sea Change

When I sat transfixed in my room on High Street in Exeter, New Hampshire, in the late 1940s, listening to *The Lone Ranger* on my radio, I had no idea where my dawning interest in horses would lead me over the next seven decades.

As I mentioned at the beginning of this book, I had my first real beginning a few years later, after my parents took over the running of the Stoneleigh Prospect Hill School for Girls in Greenfield, Massachusetts. We moved there in the late summer of 1950, just after my ninth birthday, and suddenly there was a real barn filled with real horses a 30-second walk from my back door.

That first beginning was on a little pinto pony who came from a dealer, complete with a Western saddle and bridle. Three years later, when I'd outgrown Paint, I rode my new horse, Bonfire, named after a Walter Farley trotter, in a bigger Western saddle, but I also started to ride him English so that I could enter more classes at the local shows, and win more ribbons.

Then I rode in the 1956 GMHA 100-mile trail ride, a rather big new direction. Then, in 1956, I got my first Morgan, Lippitt Sandy, a bigger new direction.

And so on, over the following decades: new horses, new types of riding, new teachers, new adventures, new directions, to the point where trying something new was normal.

But all along, during all the experimentation, the reinventions, the various competitive successes, I was held back by the way I had been taught to regard the essential relationship between humans and horses when I was nine, 10, 11, and 12—those formative years when you begin to solidify your assumptions of what is true or false.

At the heart of what I now recognize as a "fundamental truth" that turned out to be not true was the idea that a horse was an underling in the partnership and should be "made to do as he is told." It was the conventional wisdom of the adults who first taught me: the human was the boss, and the horse had to be made to obey.

If I delve deeper into this concept, I think the underlying challenge rises from the fact that we have two species, humans and horses—the human, basically a meat-eating predator, and the horse, a grass-eating creature of prey—and we are asking them to form a working partnership. I mean, really, what could possibly go wrong?

I am not trying to justify why it took me so long to realize that it was my role as the human to sublimate my dominance, except to point out that there are lots of blue ribbons, gold medals, fame and fortune being won and celebrated by humans who do force horses into compliance, and I realize that I accepted that without question for far too long.

But at some point it began to nag at me, the idea that my horses had to be underlings in the partnership, and the underlying truth was that I had little comprehension of training methods that didn't employ force. And, sure, I had a USET gold medal, I had been USET National Three-Day Champion a couple of times, USCTA "Rider of the Year"—but without realizing it back then, I was what I now consider a bad trainer, because when things got tough, I got tougher.

Born in 1941, brought up learning to ride in the 1950s, a time when the conventional wisdom was, "You've got to show that horse who's boss," I was still drinking that Kool-Aid.

But I sensed intuitively that I was in a trap, and that making a horse do something started a downward spiral, but I didn't know how to escape. My biggest, most essentially honest reinvention was still in the future as recently as 20 years ago. It might never have happened if I hadn't been uncomfortable enough to realize something needed to change. I found myself actively searching for a new, gentler approach.

It was too slow a process for me, changing from a hard way to a quieter way. For anyone who is struggling as I was, I'll share some things that helped.

One day, I happened to read about a training concept bound up in the German word *losgelassenheit*, and while I may not have grasped its essence, I did grasp a key part.

The concept of *losgelassenheit* involves training in a state of looseness, but it isn't really that so much as it is training in an absence of tightness. So then I thought, "Wait a minute. There is physical tightness and emotional tightness. If I am going to avoid emotional tightness as well, it logically follows that I can't do things that make my horse tense. A tense horse doesn't learn." Duh. I was beginning to see that.

My next step was to begin to try to understand what is actually meant by the term "aids." As we've discussed already, aids are basically nonverbal communications, applied not with vocal cords but with pressures and releases from seat, hands, legs, weight distribution. Each set of pressures and releases means something specific and different to the horse, just as the word C-A-T to a young child learning to read means something different from D-O-G.

So any aid applied strongly enough to create nervous tension is an aid applied too strongly. *There's part of my problem*, I realized. A kick tells the horse what I want, but it *also* creates tension, so I have to teach my horse to respond instead to a nudge, a tickle, some pressure that allows him to stay below his anxiety threshold.

Everything I had been doing was based on too much—too much force, too much pressure, too much too soon, too much assumption that my horse knew what I wanted but was simply not doing it right, too much, too much. I wasn't teaching, I was forcing. And force *always* escalates, because force creates anxiety in the horse, anxiety creates resistance, resistance elicits more force from the rider to counteract it, and down the rabbit hole we go.

This is a long and somewhat complex description of what I consider to be my "best" reinvention, but it is a fundamental truth that I wish I had learned half a century earlier, and if it can help some riders and trainers—at any age—on their journey, I believe it will help them create stronger bonds with their horses.

Field Notes

Horses, Humans, and the Idea of Becoming an Athlete

Horses are just horses. In a wild herd setting they eat, drink, reproduce, wander to find sustenance, play when they feel like it, perhaps run from perceived threats, but they don't have agendas the way humans do, so they don't get up in the morning thinking, "What can I do today to become a stronger, fitter, more successful athlete?"

Some humans do that. We have systematic levels of sports: peewee league, little league, junior varsity, varsity, all the levels above those leading to such institutions as major league sports, the world championships, and the Olympic Games. Humans celebrate successful athletes in hundreds of ways—newspaper mentions, magazine covers, sponsorships, endorsements, salaries, glory, fame, medals, ribbons, recognition, adulation. It can become its own sort of narcotic.

Most of us no longer use horses for transportation or for farm work, so we have invented various sports as substitute ways to enjoy being around them. To make sure that the horse side of the partnership isn't being taken advantage of, we train them carefully, and compete them at levels within their abilities. Here at Huntington Farm, Randy Ward and another rider are warming up before cross-country. There are dozens of horse sports. This one is called "eventing" and was originally created as a test of military officers and their horses. ▼

So now we have this strange partnership between human and horse. It is strange in that only one of the two partners, the human, has an agenda beyond doing as little hard work as possible and getting through the day safely and without undue stress. The horse has no interest in medals, fame, glory. The saying is that a horse's gold is green, as in green grass. But the human, if competitive, needs to turn the horse into an athlete to be able to do well. So right here is where it can get dicey.

How can the agenda-driven human bring a member of a grazing, creature-of-flight species along in that quest—in ways that are humane

Denny Emerson | *Begin and Begin Again*

and fair—when half of the partnership couldn't give a darn? Can the human have enough empathy to stay within the bounds of kindness, or will the drive to victory blind the human past the point of good horsemanship, if we agree that the definition of a good horseman is something like, "Someone who, in an educated way, always puts the best interests of the horse first and foremost"? ◆

_ Kansas: Developing a Working Relationship

Here's a real-life example of how that sea change in my thinking brought about better results: I was recently riding my son Rett's Quarter Horse Kansas, formerly a ranch horse and team roping horse. Kansas is a good example, because he's in his teens and has become used to doing certain things in certain ways—in his case, little contact on longer reins. The same thing would apply to a former racehorse, or a former Park Morgan, or any horse that has long-established patterns of response.

When I ask Kansas for even a little bit of contact, legs into connection, his first responses are to evade, dip his head, open his mouth, invert, basically telling me the only way that he knows how, "Hey, I don't get what you want. Hey, this isn't comfortable for me to do." So I stay very quiet, and simply suggest. And I understand how hard it must be for Kansas, so if I am going to make any changes, they will be tiny changes, done over plenty of time, with plenty of releases and rest breaks. I may not even go much further than slight contact, just to steady him from time to time, because he's so used to a certain pattern. I'm not trying to change Kansas into something he isn't, not at this stage of his life.

I was thinking recently of how I might have responded 25 or 30 years ago, and I am pretty sure that I'd have been more demanding and more inclined to think of Kansas's evasions as "disobediences" rather than as struggles. And I know that many trainers find themselves in these situations, and think, as I once did, that since the horse is not "doing what I ask," he must be somehow acting badly, and that at some level he knows what I want but simply is being a brat about it. The moment the rider's mind goes there, it starts a confrontational downward spiral, as the rider feels the evasion, misinterprets its cause, becomes more demanding—and you know the drill from there.

I was trying to think of ways to explain, in human terms, what I think Kansas, and all the hundreds of thousands of other horses like him, are feeling.

Take a human sport like figure skating, gymnastics, skiing, and think of how, if you were being asked to do those movements, your body would be unable to comply. You don't have the feel for it, you are not used to it, you don't have the elasticity nor the strength nor the balance to be able to do it. If you were going to become proficient, it would take you years, beginning with the most basic baby steps, and, little by little, you would start to become able to perform in different ways. We know this, right?

Yes, we do, if we apply it to ourselves, and yet there are plenty of trainers—and I was one of them—who would feel those inabilities in a horse, misinterpret the root cause, and start to ramp up the pressure. Some even use draw-reins, harsh bits, drugs; some know no limits to what they will do to force compliance from horses, and this is, sometimes, because they are harsh humans, but more often because they don't know any other way, and are frustrated.

"What is the way forward?" one might ask, as I did. Well, better education, that's part of it, but most important, being willing and open enough to accept this education. That can be challenging, especially if the old way is getting results, ribbons, salary checks, names in the horse magazine headlines, and photos on the covers.

It comes back to whether or not we accept that definition of a good horseman or horsewoman: "A good horseman or horse-woman is someone who, in an educated way, always puts the best interest of the horse first and foremost."

_ The Vast Mosaic

I once read a description of the world of horses as a mosaic. An actual mosaic is a great many small pieces of glass or stone or other materials of various shapes and colors, interwoven in such a way as to create some larger image.

Consider the hundreds of breeds of horses and ponies, the multitude of uses to which they are put, the vast support network surrounding horses: medicine, barns, transport, trucks, trailers, vans, dental, shoeing, saddles, books, paintings, ranches, farms, songs, associations, shows, events, trail rides, tack, supplies, clothing, boots, bridles, on and on and on.

The mosaic concept fits.

And here's the strange and wonderful reality: how any one person fits into this intricate pattern, whether that individual's connection to horses represents one little sliver of glass or dozens, is only important or valid insofar as it seems important or valid to that person. At any given moment, on any new, breaking day, we have the ability to change the shape and nature of that connection, to end one and to begin another, to modify an existing path, or to remain steady as she goes.

Remember the C.S. Lewis quote at the beginning of this book? "We can't go back and change the beginning, but we can start today and change the ending." Some of us find one path and follow it for a lifetime, while others—and I am one—change again and again.

There's a longstanding joke that catching the horse bug is like catching malaria—once you have it, it never goes away. But the form your horse obsession takes is up to you, just as mine is up to me. They are all valid. They are all of equal merit.

The point I would hope to make is that my choices and your choices are all valid as long as we adhere to the first principle of horsemanship—that whatever we choose is always in the best interest of the horse. ◈ ◈ ◆

INDEX

Page numbers in *italics* indicate illustrations.

INDEX

Page numbers
in *italics* indicate
illustrations.

INDEX

Page numbers
in *italics* indicate
illustrations.

INDEX